This Rum Tasting Log Book

Belongs to

____

DEDICATION

This Rum Tasting Log Book is dedicated to all the Rum Lovers out there who are mindful of tasty drinks and want to have fun in the process.

You are my inspiration for producing books and I'm honored to be a part of keeping all of your thoughts and ideas organized all in one easy to find spot.

How to use this Rum Tasting Log Book:

This ultimate rum tasting notebook is a perfect way to track and record all your tasty activities. This unique rum tasting journal is a great way to keep all of your important information all in one easy to find spot.

Each interior page includes prompts and space to record the following:

1. Name - Write the name of which rum you are tasting.

2. Distiller - Use the box provided to write in who made it, or what company.

3. Origin - Stay on task using the box to fill in where in the world this rum was made.

4. Color Meter- Record and track the color of the rum that is being sampled, from clear to black

5. Flavor Wheel - Checklist what flavor was sampled, anywhere from woody to spicy.

6. Additional Notes - Space to write additional thoughts and ideas.

7. Final Rating - Fill in checklist star rating from 1-5 on appearance, taste, mouthfeel and overall rating.

If you are new to tasting rum or have been at it for a while, this rum tasting journal is a must have! Can make a great useful gift for anyone that aspires to be a rum tasting sommelier!

Have Fun!

NAME	
DISTILLERY	TYPE
ORIGIN	AGE
PRICE	SAMPLED

COLOR METER

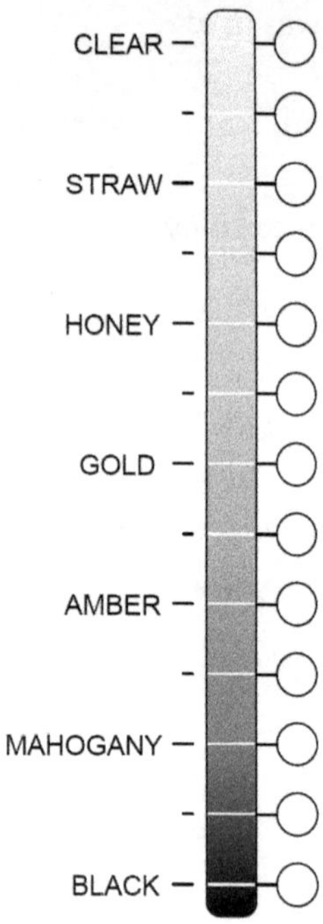

FLAVOR WHEEL

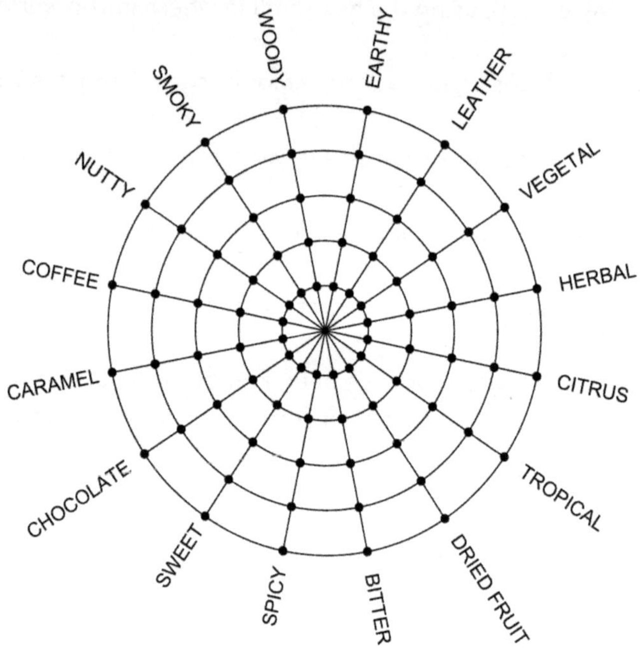

ADDITIONAL NOTES

FINAL RATING

APPEARANCE	☆☆☆☆☆
TASTE	☆☆☆☆☆
MOUTHFEEL	☆☆☆☆☆
OVERALL RATING	☆☆☆☆☆

NAME	
DISTILLERY	TYPE
ORIGIN	AGE
PRICE	SAMPLED

COLOR METER

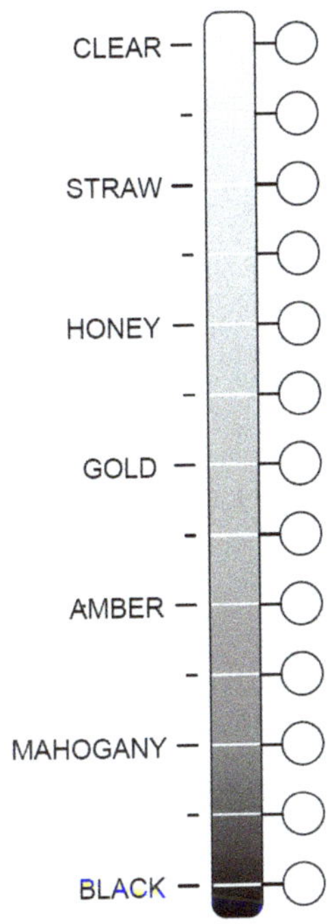

FLAVOR WHEEL

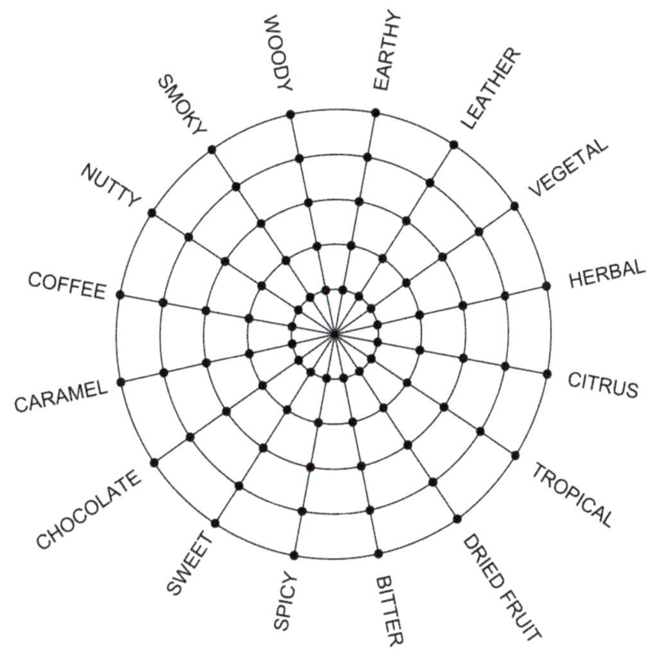

ADDITIONAL NOTES

FINAL RATING

APPEARANCE ☆☆☆☆☆

TASTE ☆☆☆☆☆

MOUTHFEEL ☆☆☆☆☆

OVERALL RATING ☆☆☆☆☆

NAME

DISTILLERY | TYPE

ORIGIN | AGE

PRICE | SAMPLED

COLOR METER

CLEAR –
–
STRAW –
–
HONEY –
–
GOLD –
–
AMBER –
–
MAHOGANY –
–
BLACK –

FLAVOR WHEEL

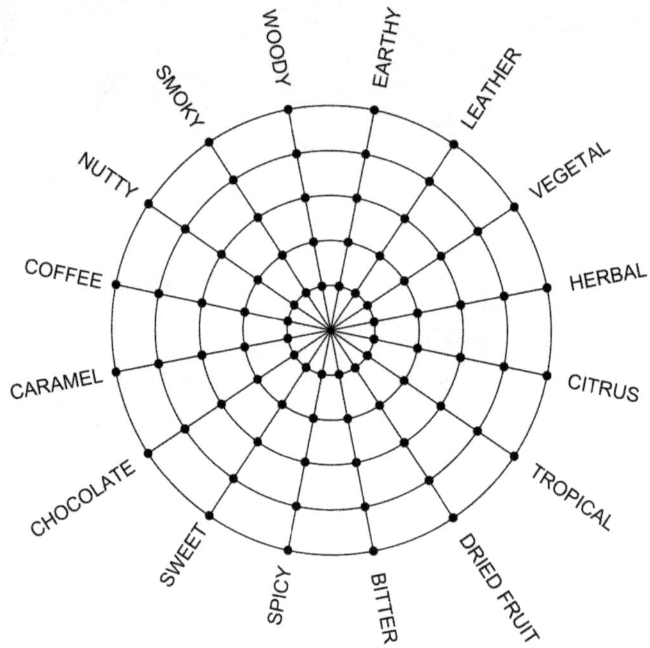

ADDITIONAL NOTES

FINAL RATING

APPEARANCE ☆☆☆☆☆

TASTE ☆☆☆☆☆

MOUTHFEEL ☆☆☆☆☆

OVERALL RATING ☆☆☆☆☆

NAME	
DISTILLERY	TYPE
ORIGIN	AGE
PRICE	SAMPLED

COLOR METER

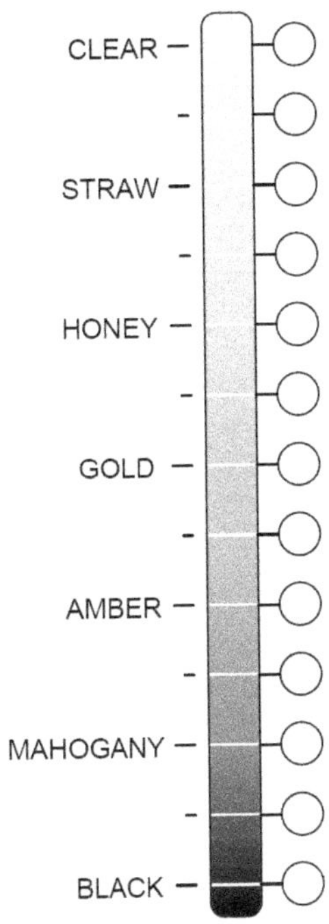

FLAVOR WHEEL

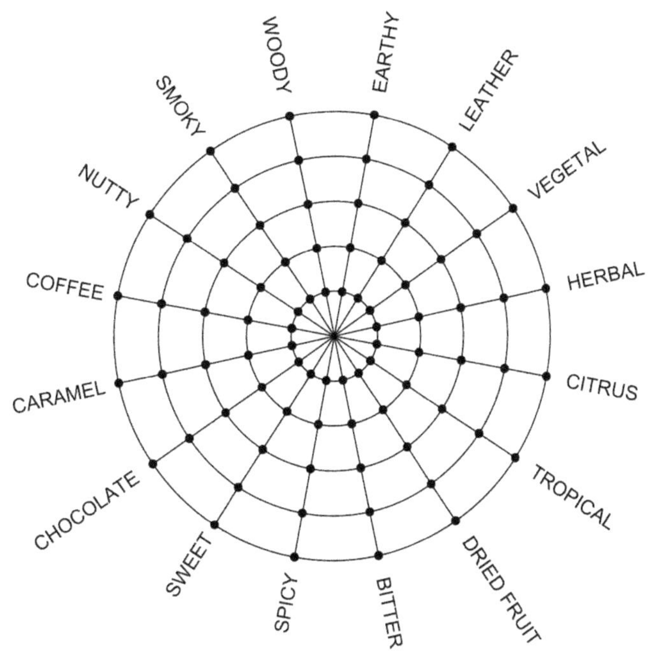

ADDITIONAL NOTES

FINAL RATING

APPEARANCE	☆☆☆☆☆
TASTE	☆☆☆☆☆
MOUTHFEEL	☆☆☆☆☆
OVERALL RATING	☆☆☆☆☆

NAME	
DISTILLERY	TYPE
ORIGIN	AGE
PRICE	SAMPLED

COLOR METER

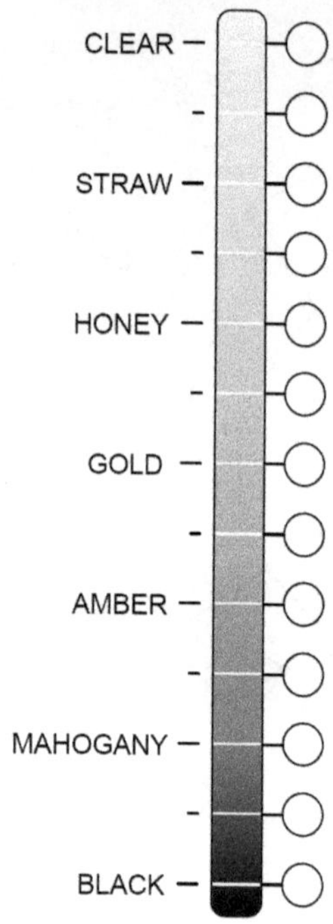

FLAVOR WHEEL

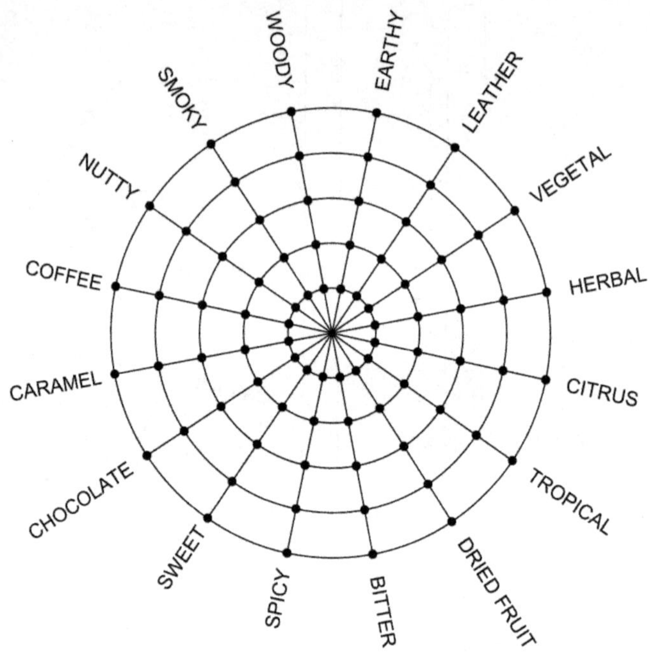

ADDITIONAL NOTES

FINAL RATING

APPEARANCE	☆☆☆☆☆
TASTE	☆☆☆☆☆
MOUTHFEEL	☆☆☆☆☆
OVERALL RATING	☆☆☆☆☆

NAME

DISTILLERY	TYPE
ORIGIN	AGE
PRICE	SAMPLED

COLOR METER

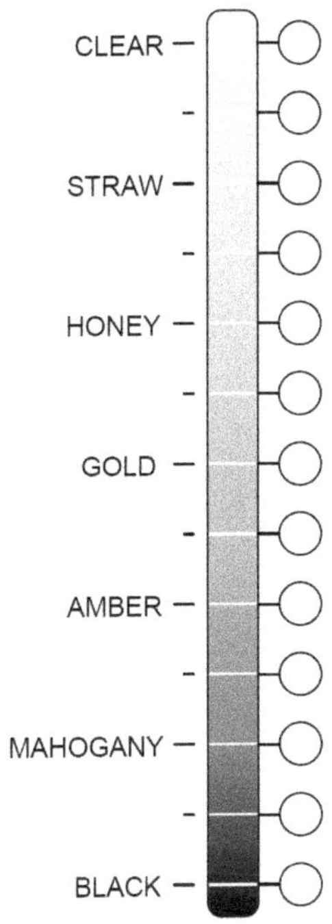

FLAVOR WHEEL

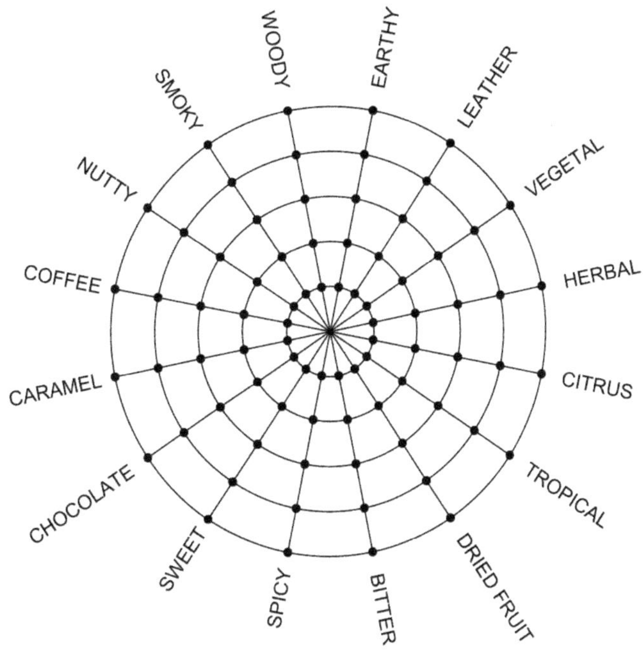

ADDITIONAL NOTES

FINAL RATING

APPEARANCE ☆☆☆☆☆

TASTE ☆☆☆☆☆

MOUTHFEEL ☆☆☆☆☆

OVERALL RATING ☆☆☆☆☆

NAME	
DISTILLERY	TYPE
ORIGIN	AGE
PRICE	SAMPLED

COLOR METER

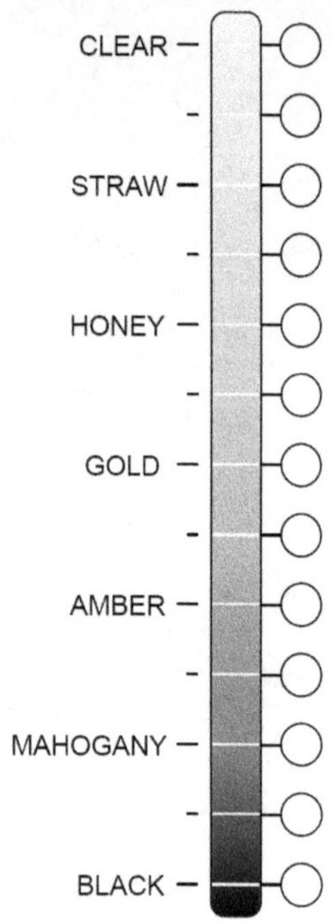

FLAVOR WHEEL

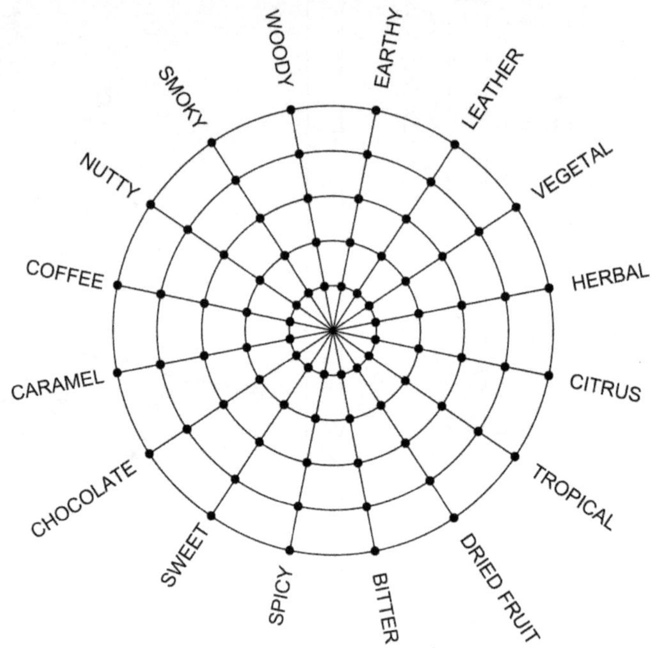

ADDITIONAL NOTES

FINAL RATING

APPEARANCE ☆☆☆☆☆

TASTE ☆☆☆☆☆

MOUTHFEEL ☆☆☆☆☆

OVERALL RATING ☆☆☆☆☆

NAME	
DISTILLERY	TYPE
ORIGIN	AGE
PRICE	SAMPLED

COLOR METER

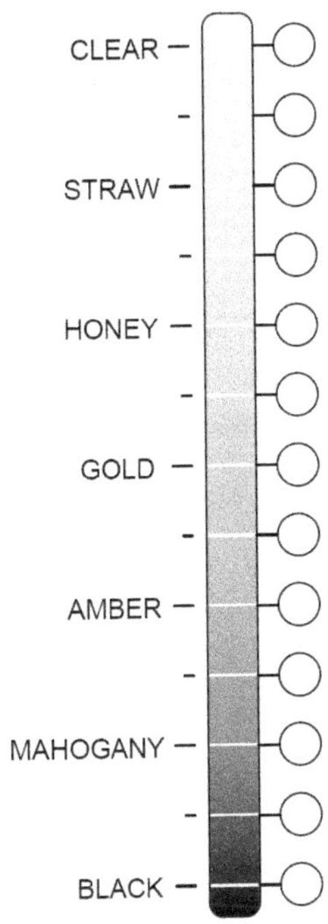

FLAVOR WHEEL

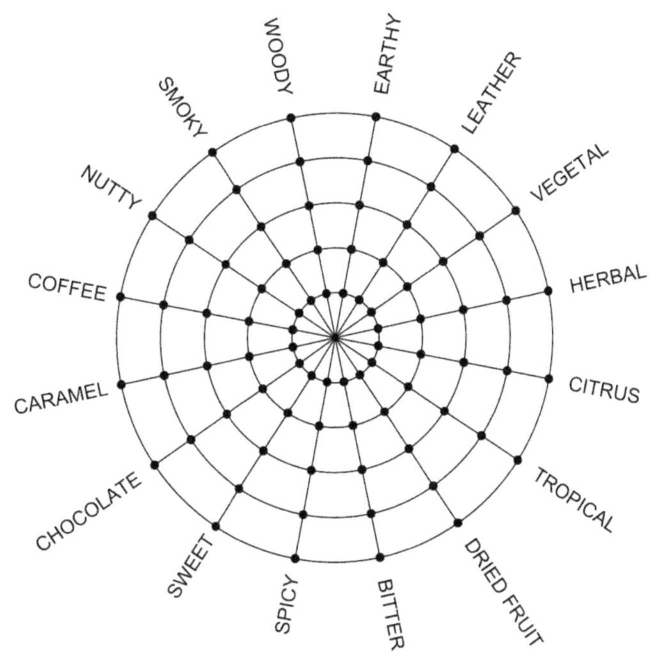

ADDITIONAL NOTES

FINAL RATING

APPEARANCE ☆☆☆☆☆

TASTE ☆☆☆☆☆

MOUTHFEEL ☆☆☆☆☆

OVERALL RATING ☆☆☆☆☆

NAME

DISTILLERY

TYPE

ORIGIN

AGE

PRICE

SAMPLED

COLOR METER

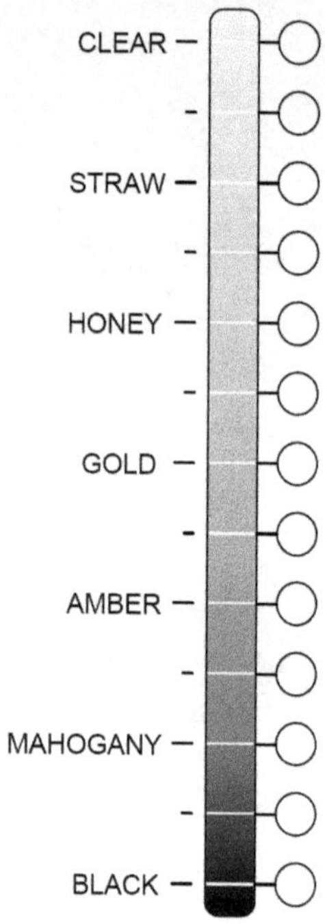

FLAVOR WHEEL

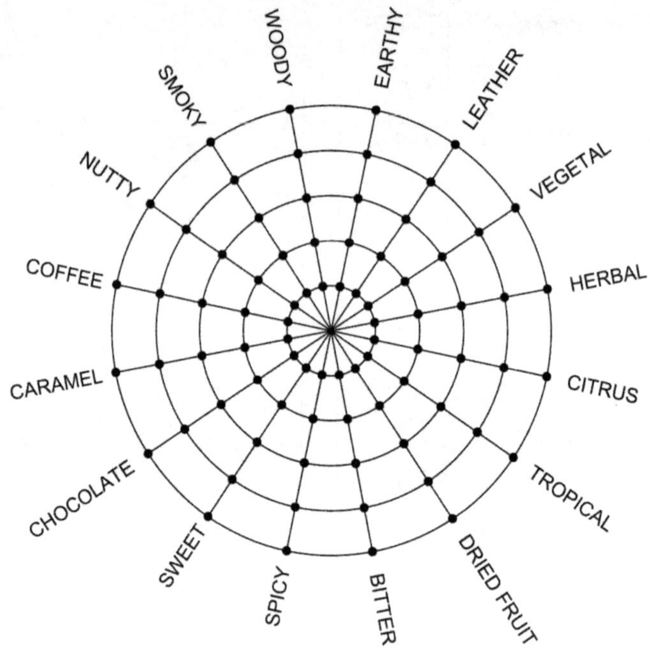

ADDITIONAL NOTES

FINAL RATING

APPEARANCE	☆☆☆☆☆
TASTE	☆☆☆☆☆
MOUTHFEEL	☆☆☆☆☆
OVERALL RATING	☆☆☆☆☆

NAME	
DISTILLERY	TYPE
ORIGIN	AGE
PRICE	SAMPLED

COLOR METER

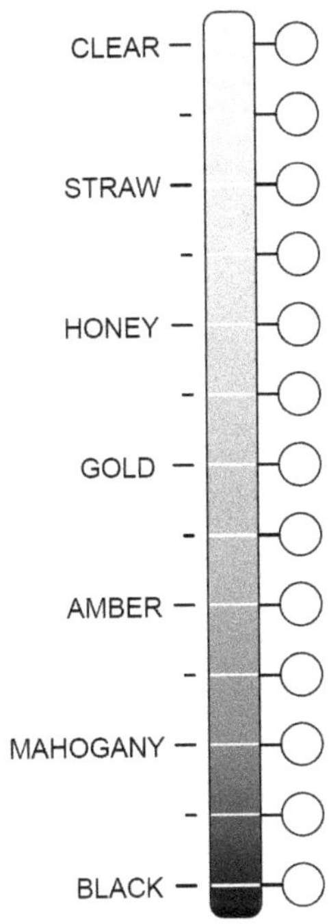

FLAVOR WHEEL

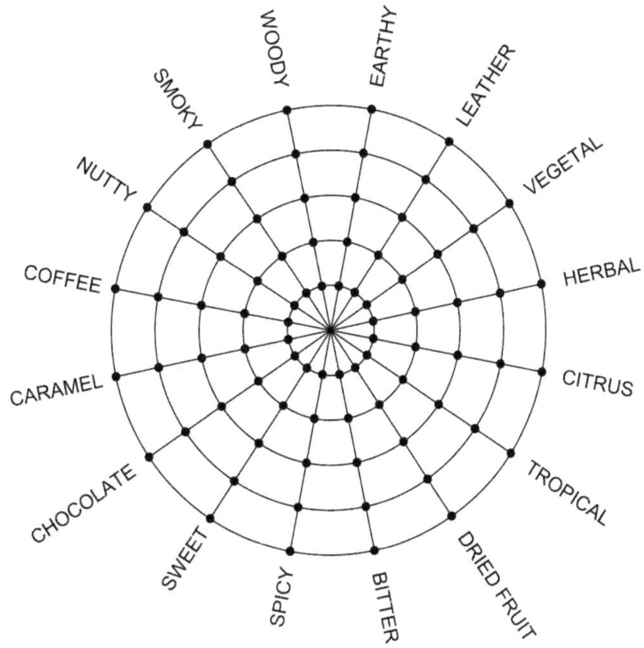

ADDITIONAL NOTES

FINAL RATING

APPEARANCE	☆☆☆☆☆
TASTE	☆☆☆☆☆
MOUTHFEEL	☆☆☆☆☆
OVERALL RATING	☆☆☆☆☆

NAME	
DISTILLERY	TYPE
ORIGIN	AGE
PRICE	SAMPLED

COLOR METER

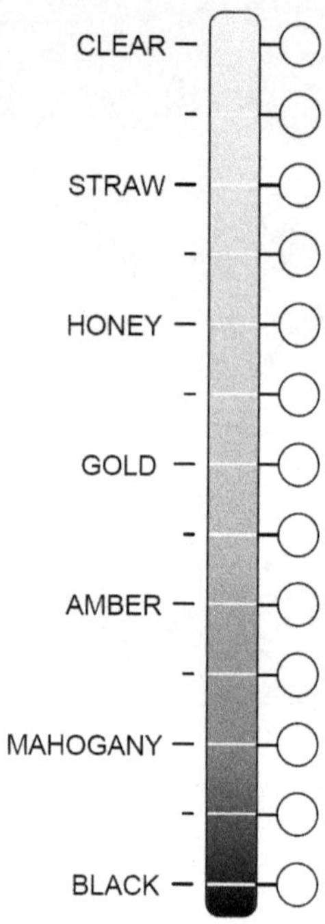

FLAVOR WHEEL

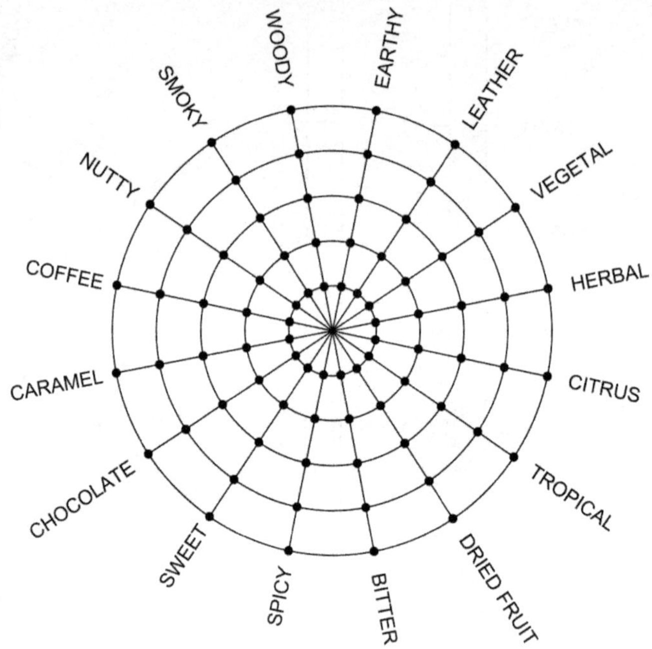

ADDITIONAL NOTES

FINAL RATING

APPEARANCE	☆☆☆☆☆
TASTE	☆☆☆☆☆
MOUTHFEEL	☆☆☆☆☆
OVERALL RATING	☆☆☆☆☆

NAME	
DISTILLERY	TYPE
ORIGIN	AGE
PRICE	SAMPLED

COLOR METER

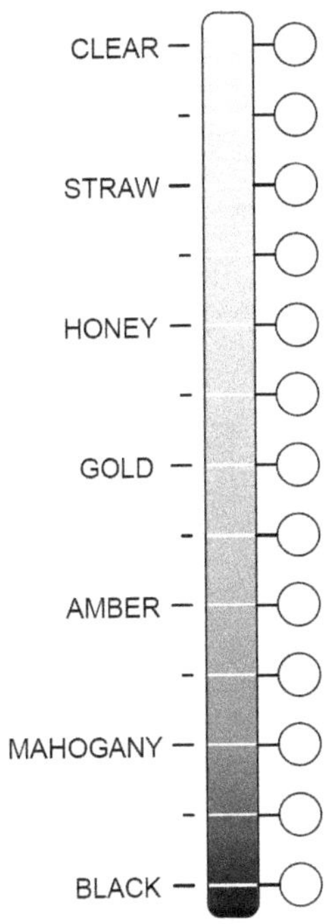

FLAVOR WHEEL

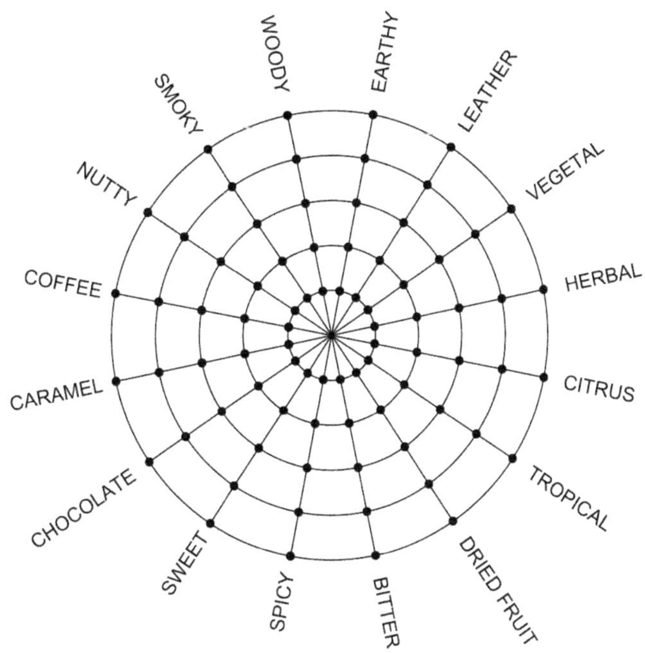

ADDITIONAL NOTES

FINAL RATING

APPENDANCE ☆☆☆☆☆

TASTE ☆☆☆☆☆

MOUTHFEEL ☆☆☆☆☆

OVERALL RATING ☆☆☆☆☆

NAME	
DISTILLERY	TYPE
ORIGIN	AGE
PRICE	SAMPLED

COLOR METER

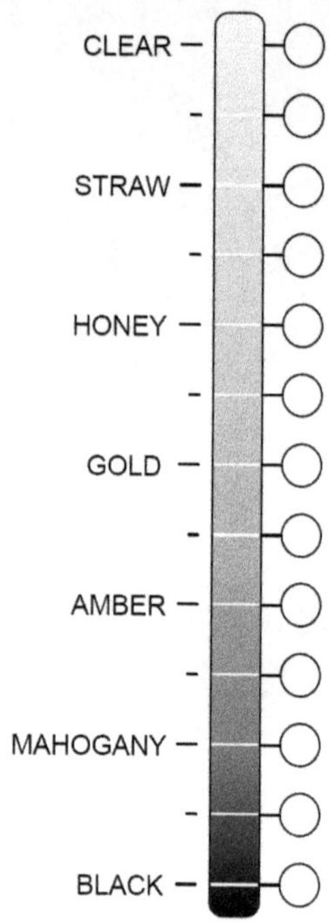

FLAVOR WHEEL

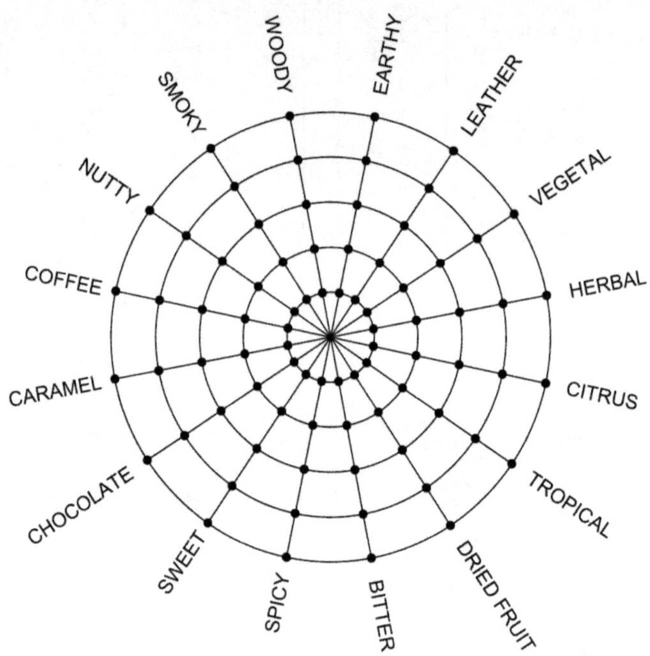

ADDITIONAL NOTES

FINAL RATING

APPEARANCE	☆☆☆☆☆
TASTE	☆☆☆☆☆
MOUTHFEEL	☆☆☆☆☆
OVERALL RATING	☆☆☆☆☆

NAME	
DISTILLERY	TYPE
ORIGIN	AGE
PRICE	SAMPLED

COLOR METER

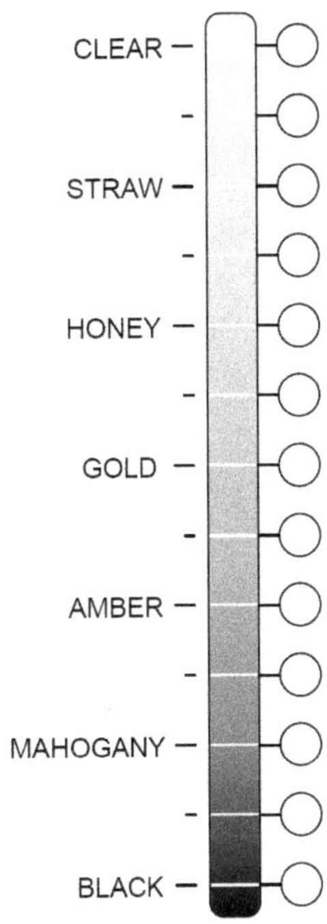

FLAVOR WHEEL

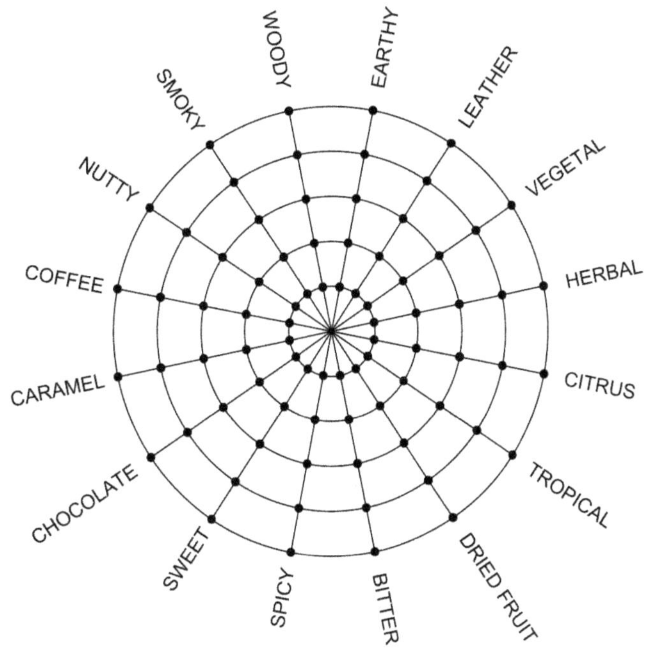

ADDITIONAL NOTES

FINAL RATING

APPEARANCE	☆☆☆☆☆
TASTE	☆☆☆☆☆
MOUTHFEEL	☆☆☆☆☆
OVERALL RATING	☆☆☆☆☆

NAME	
DISTILLERY	TYPE
ORIGIN	AGE
PRICE	SAMPLED

COLOR METER

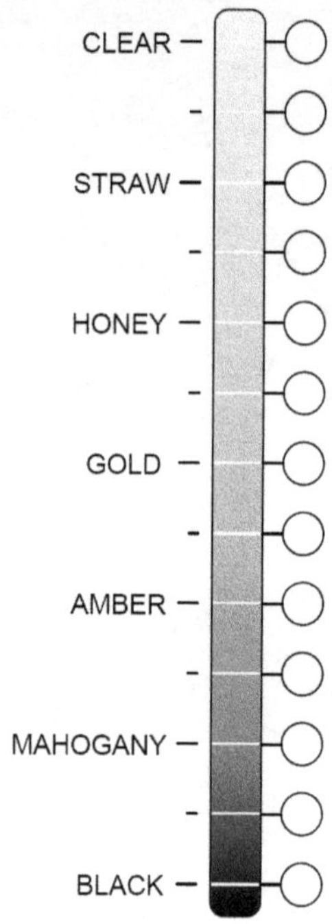

FLAVOR WHEEL

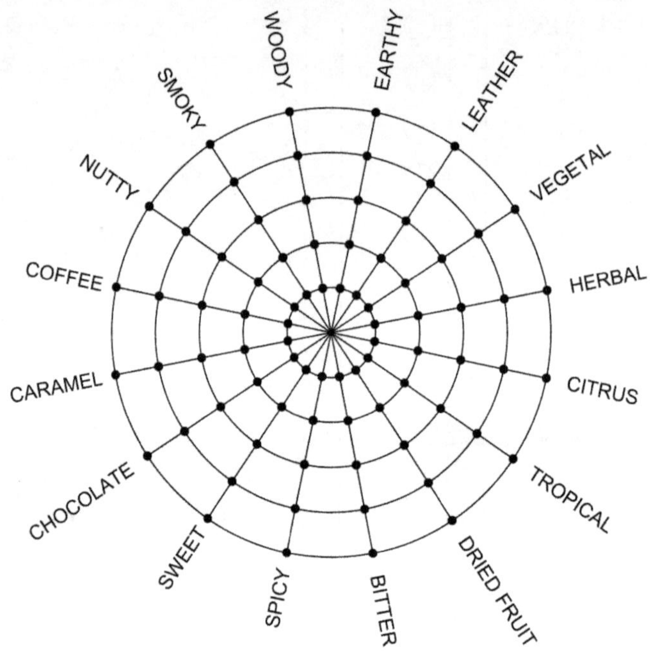

ADDITIONAL NOTES

FINAL RATING

APPEARANCE	☆☆☆☆☆
TASTE	☆☆☆☆☆
MOUTHFEEL	☆☆☆☆☆
OVERALL RATING	☆☆☆☆☆

NAME	
DISTILLERY	TYPE
ORIGIN	AGE
PRICE	SAMPLED

COLOR METER

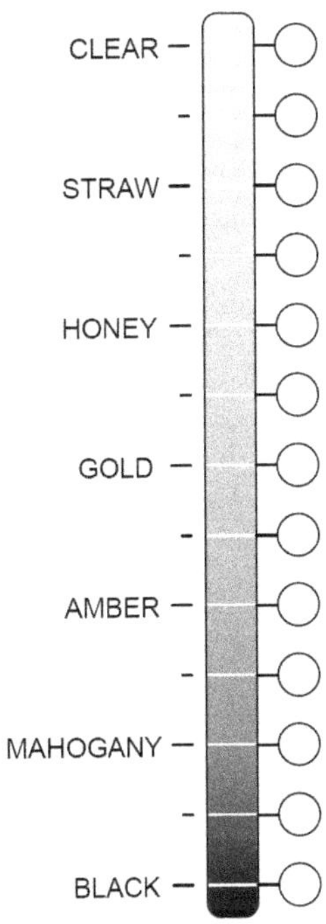

FLAVOR WHEEL

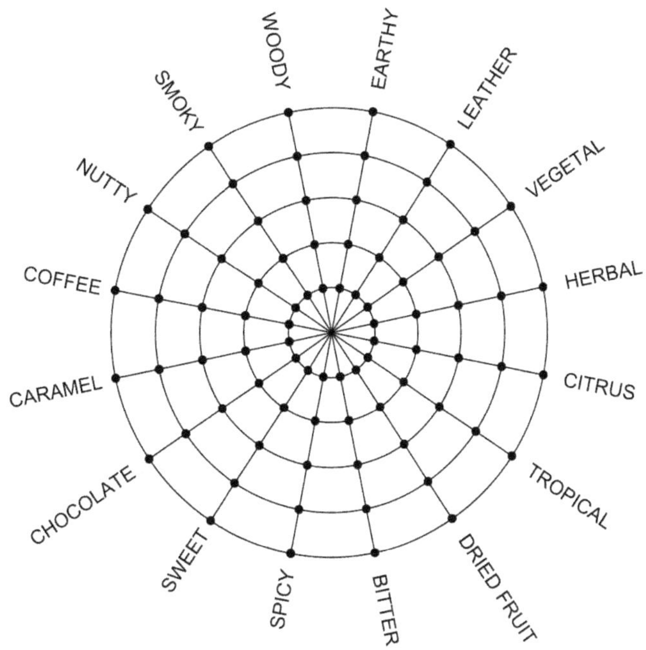

ADDITIONAL NOTES

FINAL RATING

APPEARANCE	☆☆☆☆☆
TASTE	☆☆☆☆☆
MOUTHFEEL	☆☆☆☆☆
OVERALL RATING	☆☆☆☆☆

NAME

DISTILLERY | TYPE

ORIGIN | AGE

PRICE | SAMPLED

COLOR METER

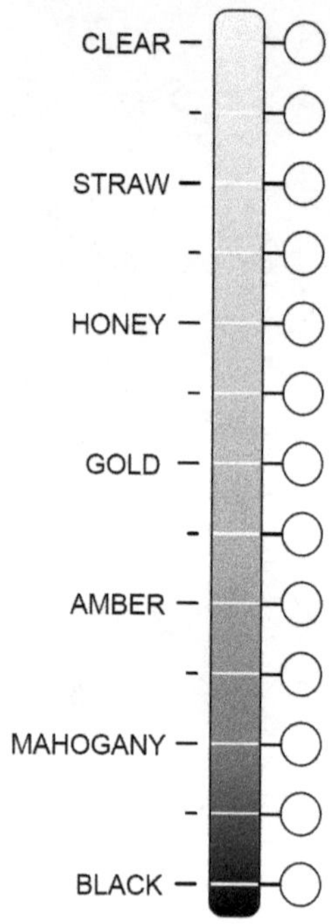

FLAVOR WHEEL

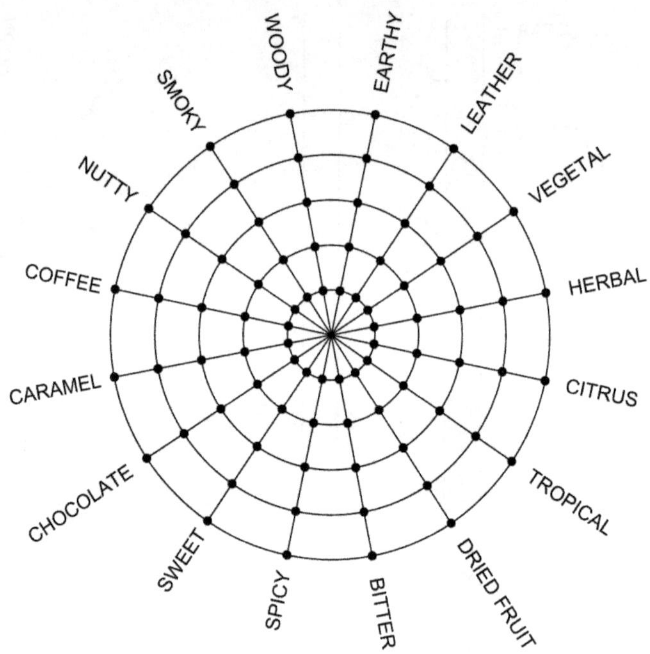

ADDITIONAL NOTES

FINAL RATING

APPEARANCE ☆☆☆☆☆

TASTE ☆☆☆☆☆

MOUTHFEEL ☆☆☆☆☆

OVERALL RATING ☆☆☆☆☆

NAME	
DISTILLERY	TYPE
ORIGIN	AGE
PRICE	SAMPLED

COLOR METER

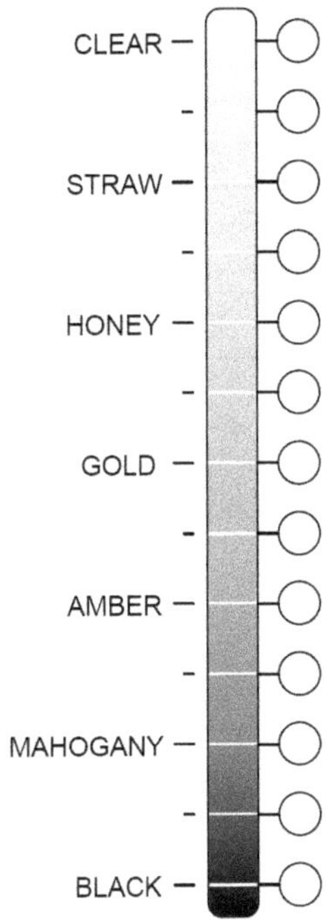

FLAVOR WHEEL

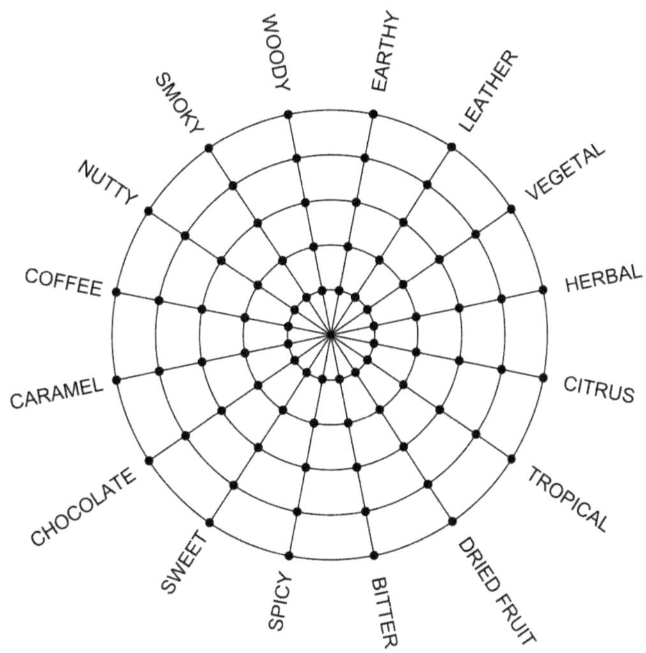

ADDITIONAL NOTES

FINAL RATING

APPEARANCE	☆☆☆☆☆
TASTE	☆☆☆☆☆
MOUTHFEEL	☆☆☆☆☆
OVERALL RATING	☆☆☆☆☆

NAME	
DISTILLERY	TYPE
ORIGIN	AGE
PRICE	SAMPLED

COLOR METER

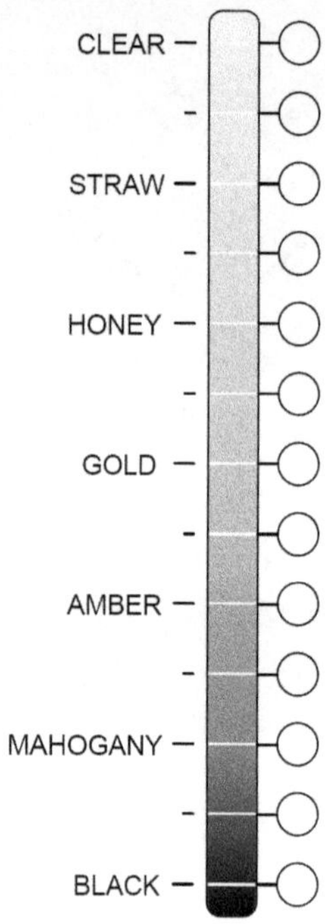

FLAVOR WHEEL

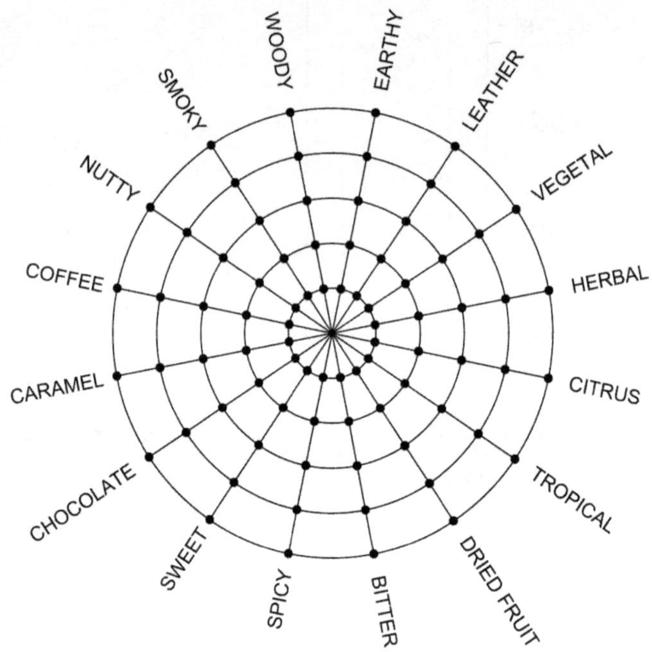

ADDITIONAL NOTES

FINAL RATING

APPEARANCE	☆☆☆☆☆
TASTE	☆☆☆☆☆
MOUTHFEEL	☆☆☆☆☆
OVERALL RATING	☆☆☆☆☆

NAME	
DISTILLERY	TYPE
ORIGIN	AGE
PRICE	SAMPLED

COLOR METER

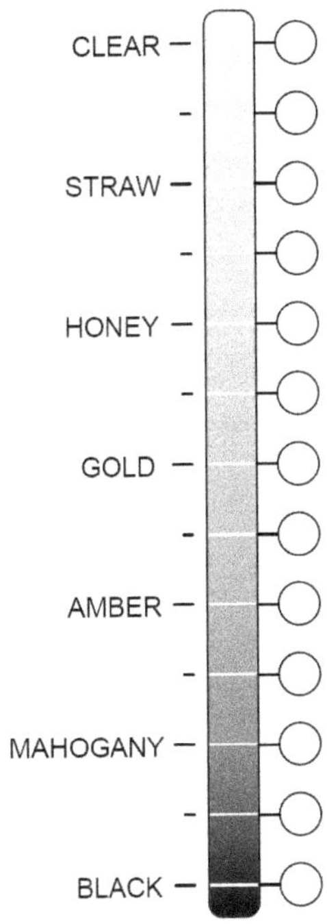

FLAVOR WHEEL

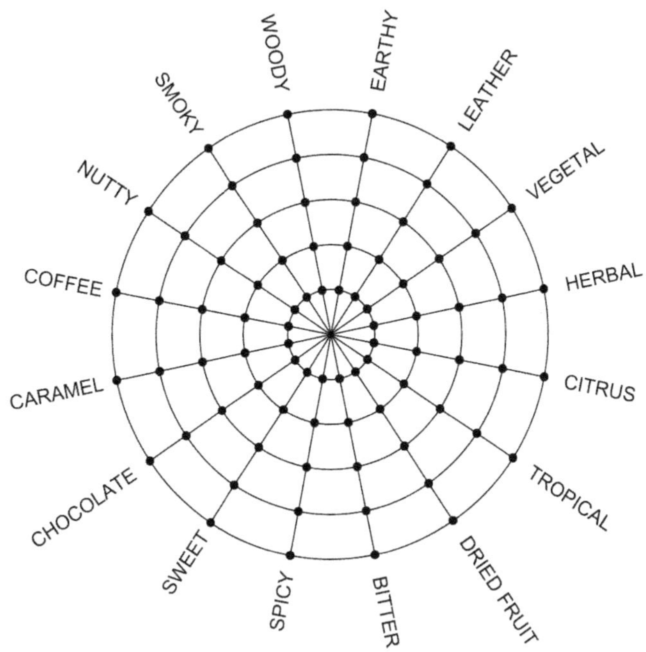

ADDITIONAL NOTES

FINAL RATING

APPEARANCE	☆☆☆☆☆
TASTE	☆☆☆☆☆
MOUTHFEEL	☆☆☆☆☆
OVERALL RATING	☆☆☆☆☆

NAME	
DISTILLERY	TYPE
ORIGIN	AGE
PRICE	SAMPLED

COLOR METER

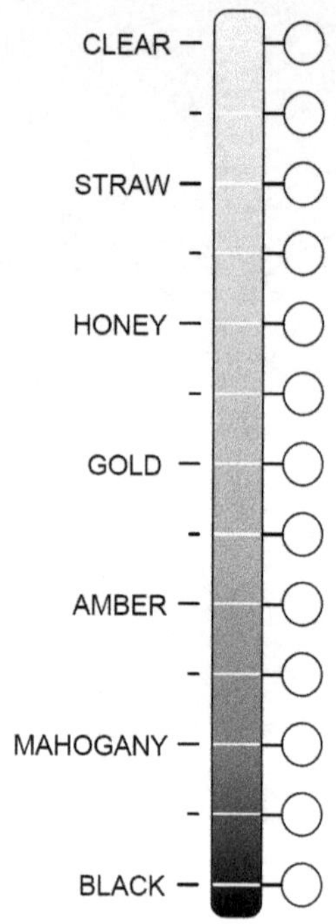

FLAVOR WHEEL

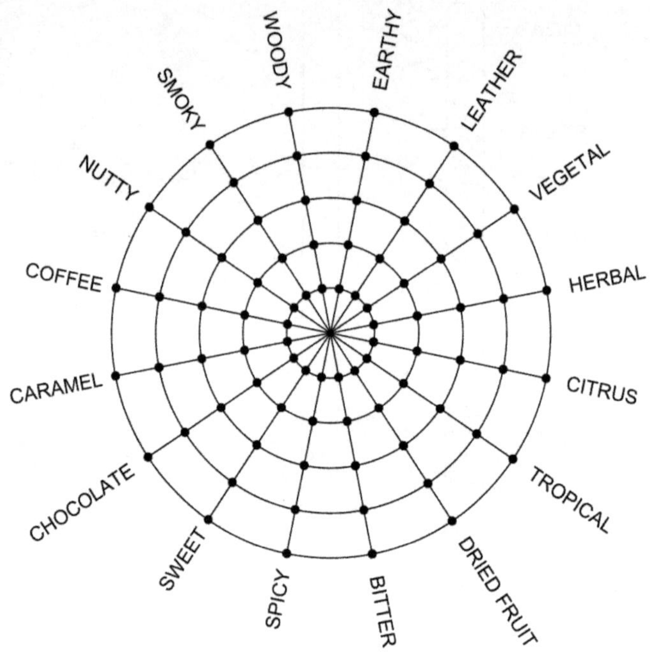

ADDITIONAL NOTES

FINAL RATING

APPEARANCE	☆☆☆☆☆
TASTE	☆☆☆☆☆
MOUTHFEEL	☆☆☆☆☆
OVERALL RATING	☆☆☆☆☆

NAME	
DISTILLERY	TYPE
ORIGIN	AGE
PRICE	SAMPLED

COLOR METER

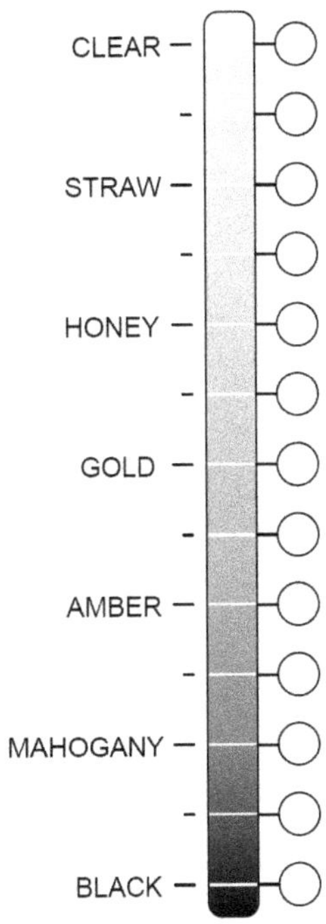

FLAVOR WHEEL

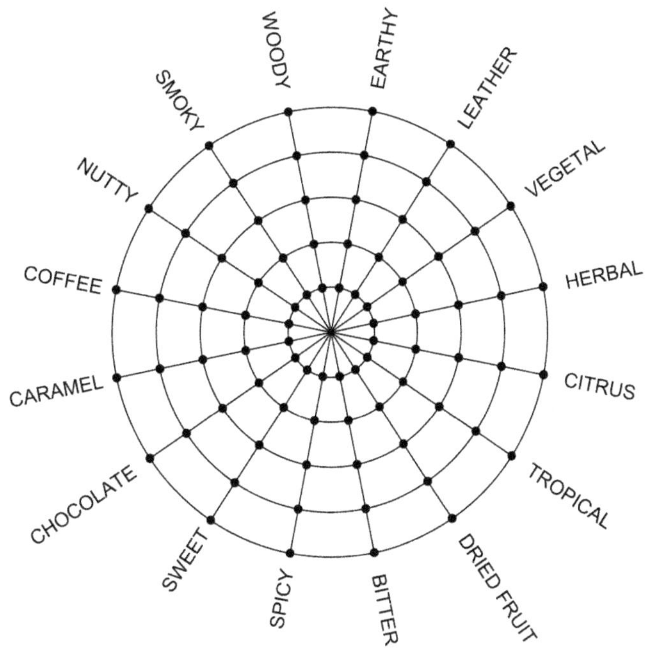

ADDITIONAL NOTES

FINAL RATING

APPEARANCE ☆☆☆☆☆

TASTE ☆☆☆☆☆

MOUTHFEEL ☆☆☆☆☆

OVERALL RATING ☆☆☆☆☆

NAME	
DISTILLERY	TYPE
ORIGIN	AGE
PRICE	SAMPLED

COLOR METER

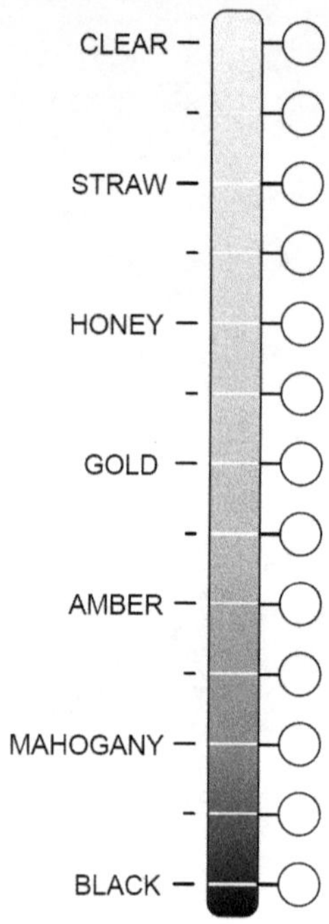

FLAVOR WHEEL

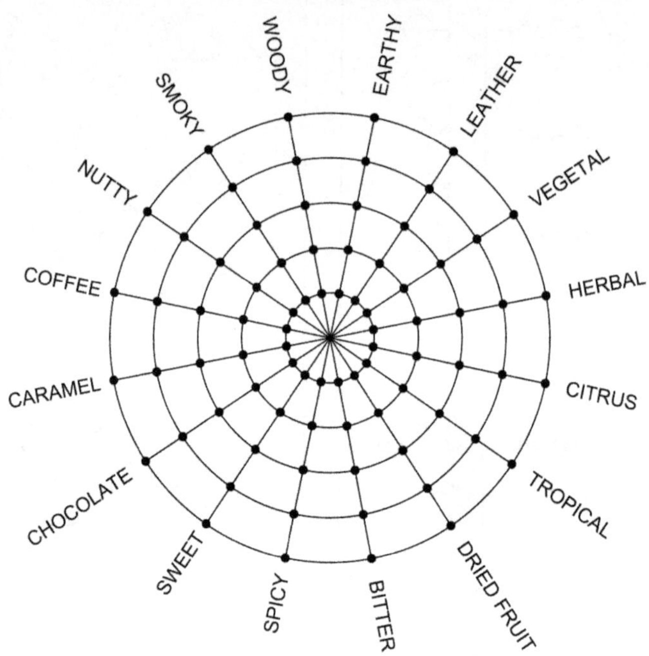

ADDITIONAL NOTES

FINAL RATING

APPEARANCE	☆☆☆☆☆
TASTE	☆☆☆☆☆
MOUTHFEEL	☆☆☆☆☆
OVERALL RATING	☆☆☆☆☆

NAME	
DISTILLERY	TYPE
ORIGIN	AGE
PRICE	SAMPLED

COLOR METER

CLEAR –
–
STRAW –
–
HONEY –
–
GOLD –
–
AMBER –
–
MAHOGANY –
–
BLACK –

FLAVOR WHEEL

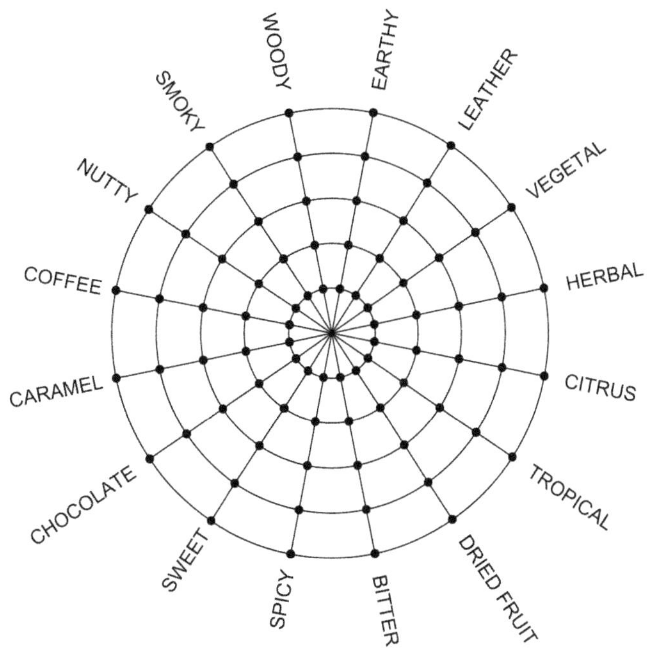

ADDITIONAL NOTES

FINAL RATING

APPEARANCE	☆☆☆☆☆
TASTE	☆☆☆☆☆
MOUTHFEEL	☆☆☆☆☆
OVERALL RATING	☆☆☆☆☆

NAME	
DISTILLERY	TYPE
ORIGIN	AGE
PRICE	SAMPLED

COLOR METER

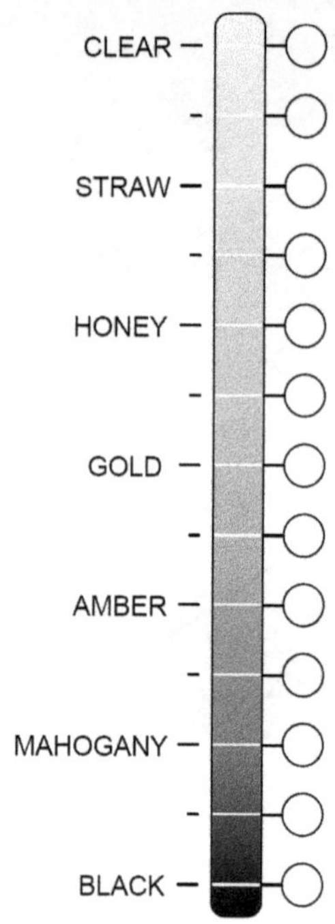

FLAVOR WHEEL

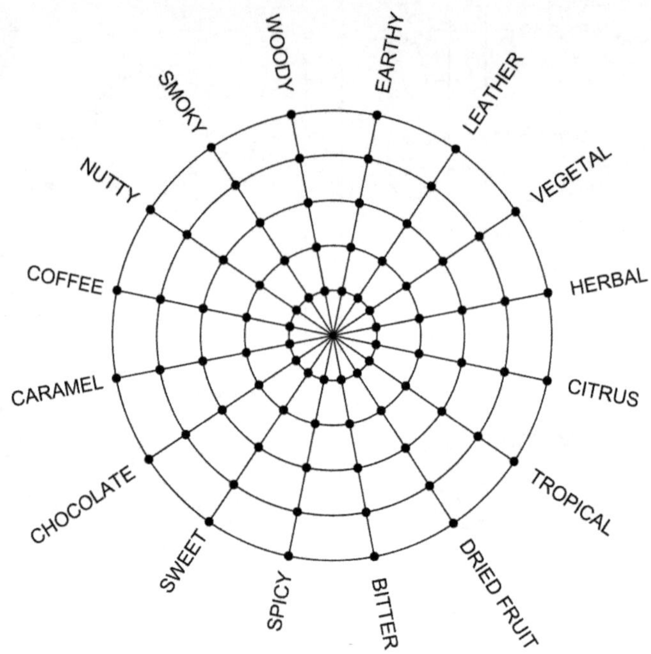

ADDITIONAL NOTES

FINAL RATING

APPEARANCE	☆☆☆☆☆
TASTE	☆☆☆☆☆
MOUTHFEEL	☆☆☆☆☆
OVERALL RATING	☆☆☆☆☆

NAME	
DISTILLERY	TYPE
ORIGIN	AGE
PRICE	SAMPLED

COLOR METER

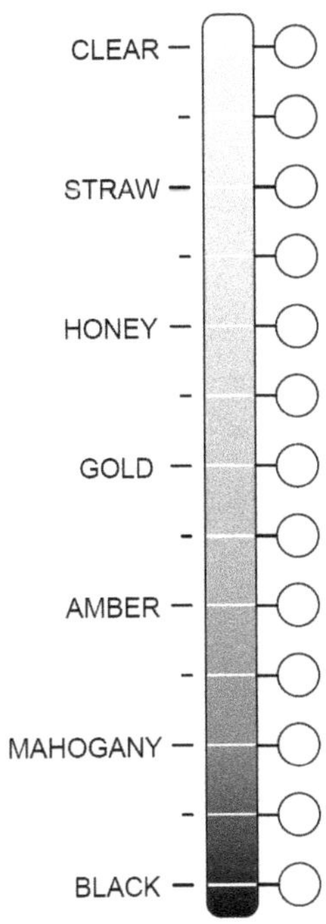

FLAVOR WHEEL

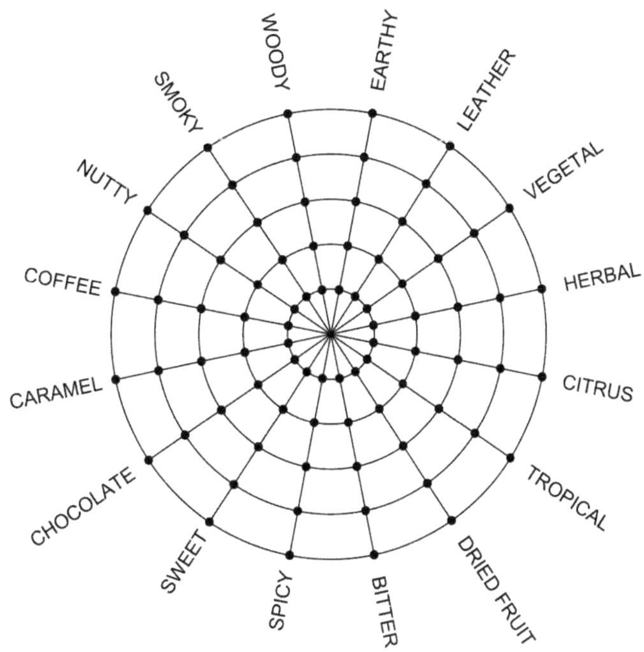

ADDITIONAL NOTES

FINAL RATING

APPEARANCE	☆☆☆☆☆
TASTE	☆☆☆☆☆
MOUTHFEEL	☆☆☆☆☆
OVERALL RATING	☆☆☆☆☆

NAME	
DISTILLERY	TYPE
ORIGIN	AGE
PRICE	SAMPLED

COLOR METER

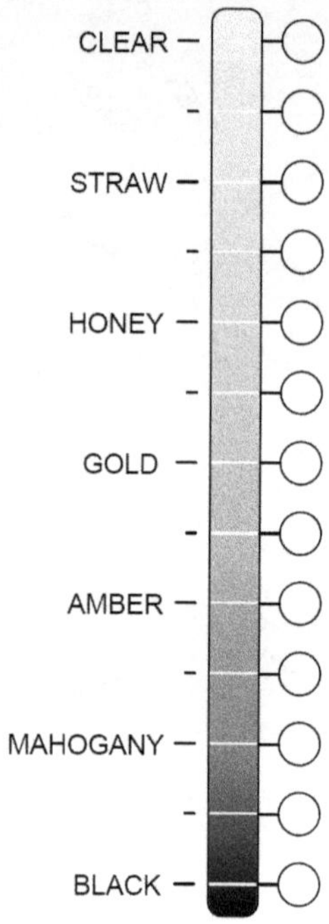

FLAVOR WHEEL

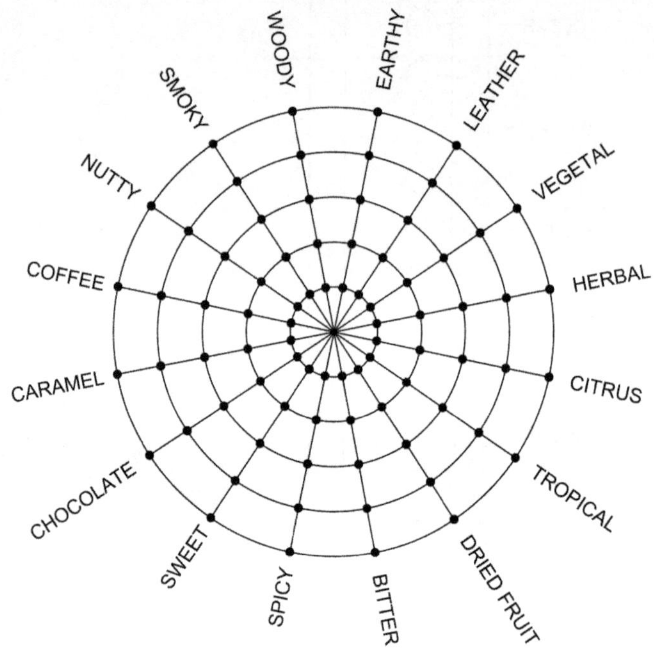

ADDITIONAL NOTES

FINAL RATING

APPEARANCE ☆☆☆☆☆

TASTE ☆☆☆☆☆

MOUTHFEEL ☆☆☆☆☆

OVERALL RATING ☆☆☆☆☆

NAME	
DISTILLERY	TYPE
ORIGIN	AGE
PRICE	SAMPLED

COLOR METER

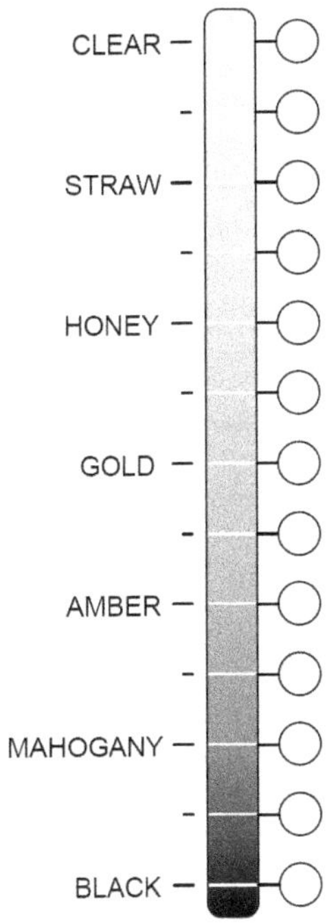

FLAVOR WHEEL

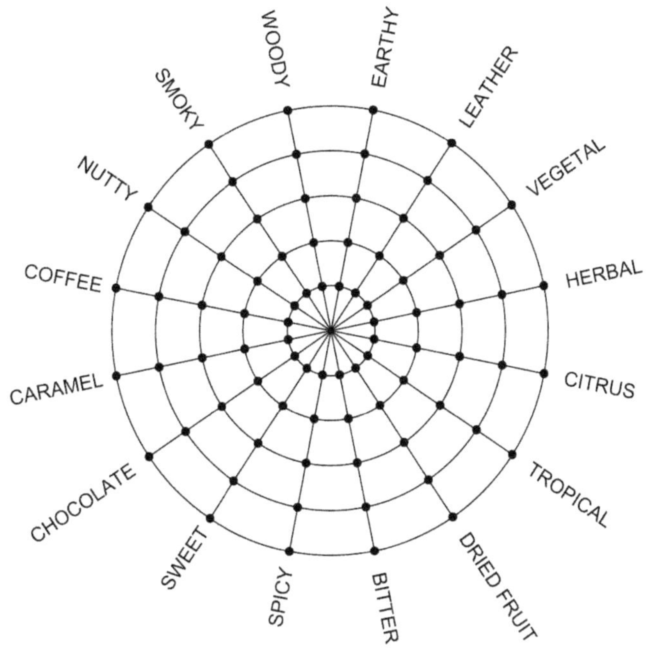

ADDITIONAL NOTES

FINAL RATING

APPEARANCE	☆☆☆☆☆
TASTE	☆☆☆☆☆
MOUTHFEEL	☆☆☆☆☆
OVERALL RATING	☆☆☆☆☆

NAME	
DISTILLERY	TYPE
ORIGIN	AGE
PRICE	SAMPLED

COLOR METER

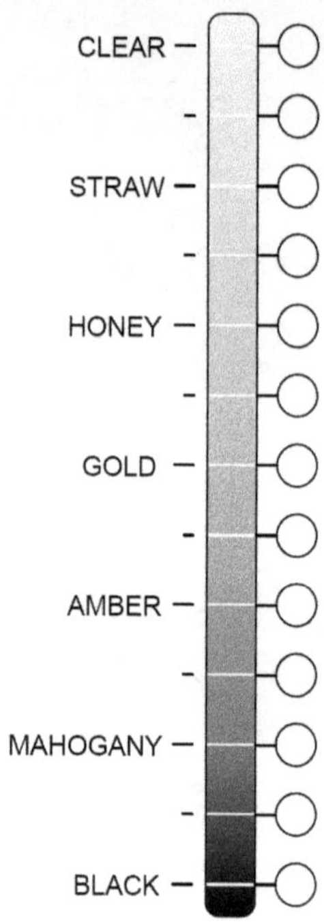

FLAVOR WHEEL

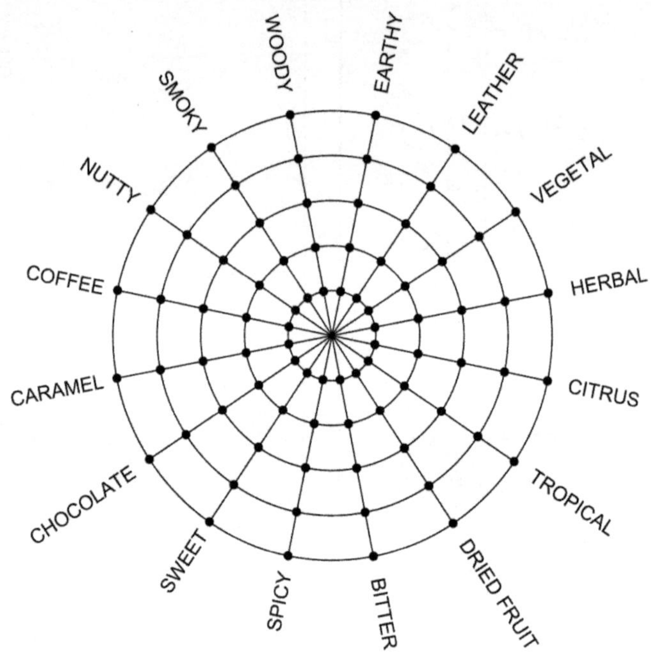

ADDITIONAL NOTES

FINAL RATING

APPEARANCE	☆☆☆☆☆
TASTE	☆☆☆☆☆
MOUTHFEEL	☆☆☆☆☆
OVERALL RATING	☆☆☆☆☆

NAME	
DISTILLERY	TYPE
ORIGIN	AGE
PRICE	SAMPLED

COLOR METER

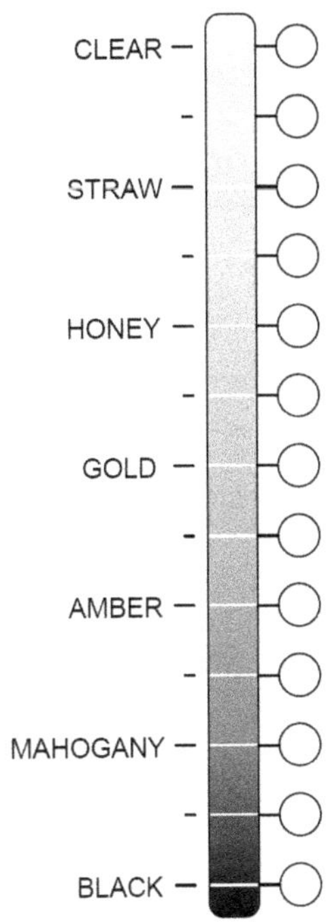

FLAVOR WHEEL

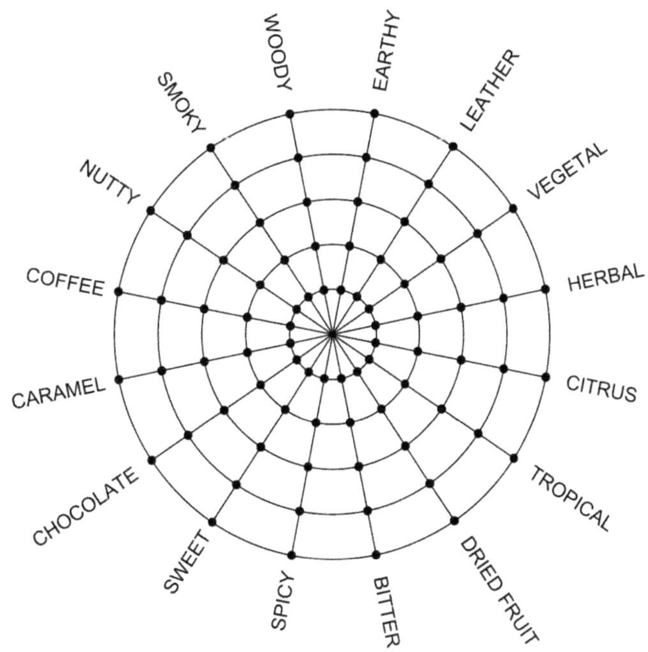

ADDITIONAL NOTES

FINAL RATING

APPEARANCE	☆☆☆☆☆
TASTE	☆☆☆☆☆
MOUTHFEEL	☆☆☆☆☆
OVERALL RATING	☆☆☆☆☆

NAME	
DISTILLERY	TYPE
ORIGIN	AGE
PRICE	SAMPLED

COLOR METER

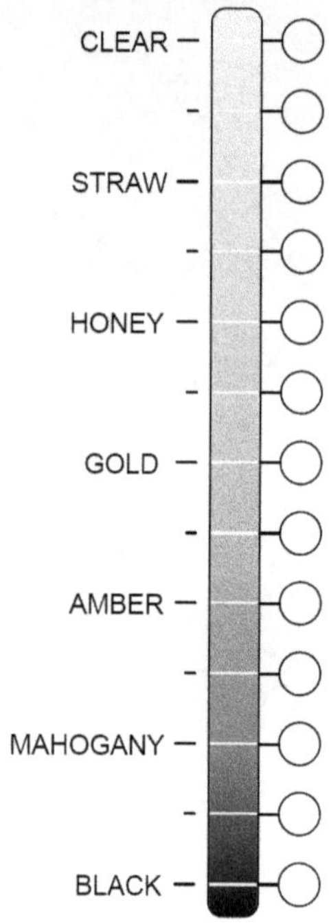

FLAVOR WHEEL

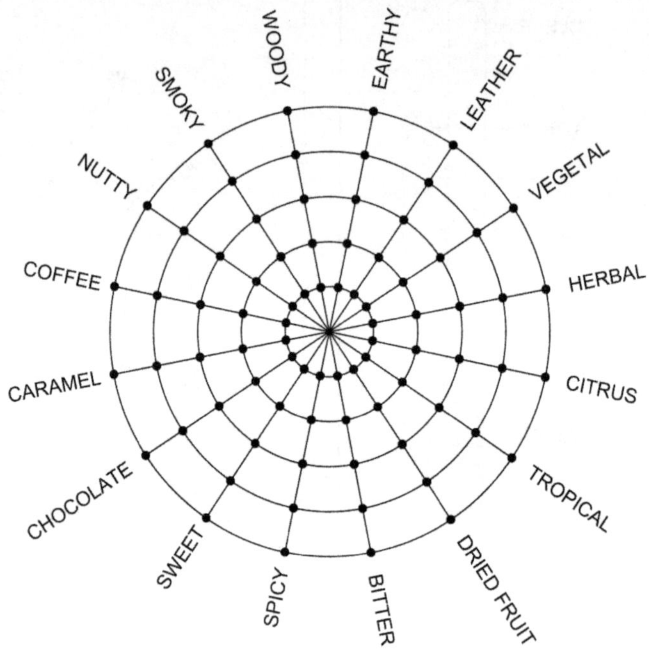

ADDITIONAL NOTES

FINAL RATING

APPEARANCE	☆☆☆☆☆
TASTE	☆☆☆☆☆
MOUTHFEEL	☆☆☆☆☆
OVERALL RATING	☆☆☆☆☆

NAME	
DISTILLERY	TYPE
ORIGIN	AGE
PRICE	SAMPLED

COLOR METER

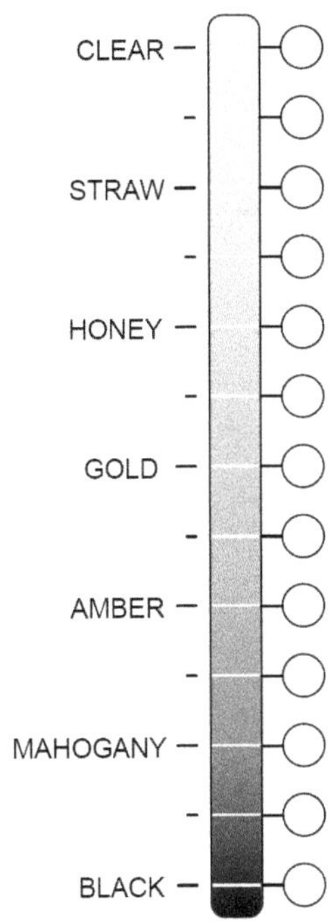

FLAVOR WHEEL

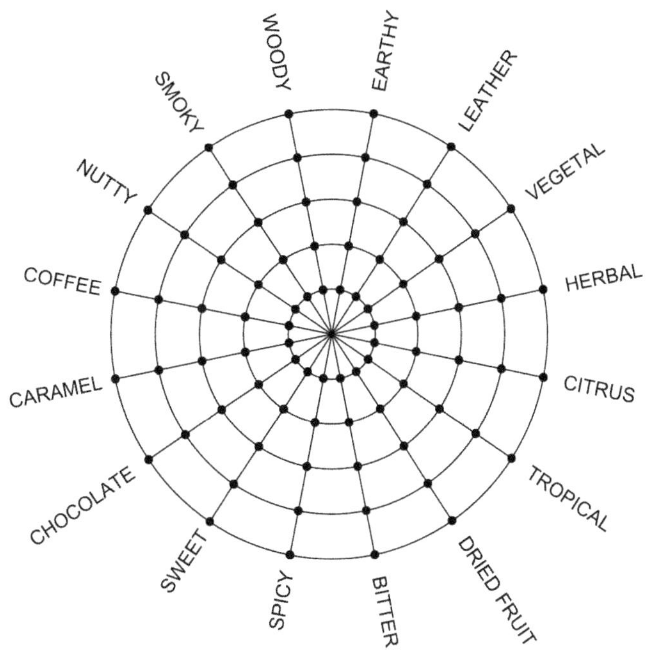

ADDITIONAL NOTES

FINAL RATING

APPEARANCE	☆☆☆☆☆
TASTE	☆☆☆☆☆
MOUTHFEEL	☆☆☆☆☆
OVERALL RATING	☆☆☆☆☆

NAME	
DISTILLERY	TYPE
ORIGIN	AGE
PRICE	SAMPLED

COLOR METER

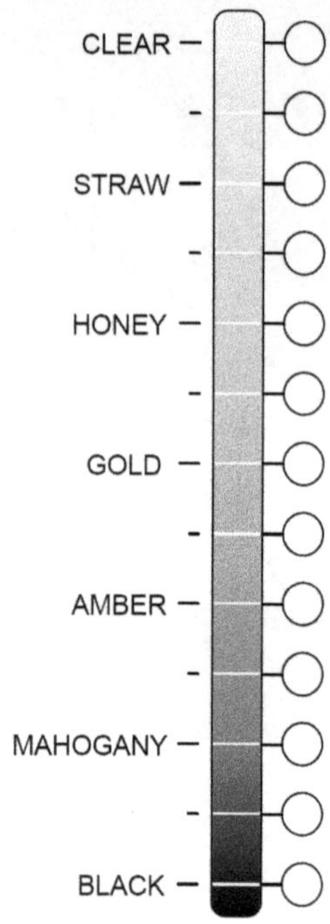

FLAVOR WHEEL

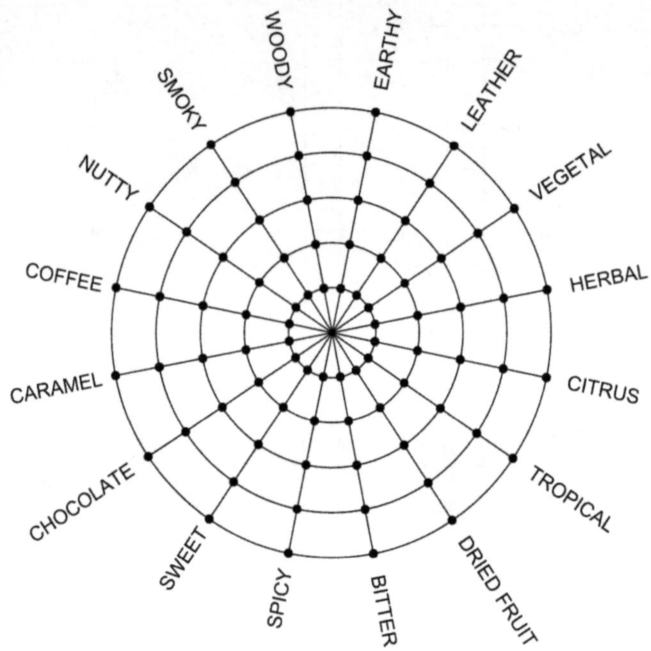

ADDITIONAL NOTES

FINAL RATING

APPEARANCE	☆☆☆☆☆
TASTE	☆☆☆☆☆
MOUTHFEEL	☆☆☆☆☆
OVERALL RATING	☆☆☆☆☆

NAME

DISTILLERY

TYPE

ORIGIN

AGE

PRICE

SAMPLED

COLOR METER

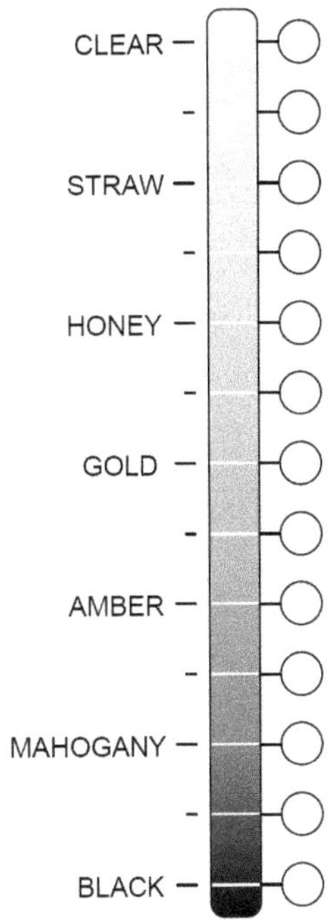

FLAVOR WHEEL

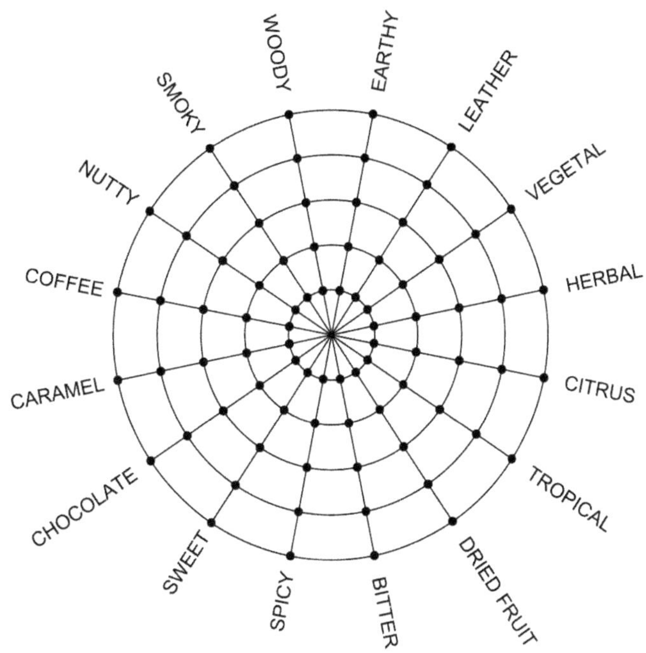

ADDITIONAL NOTES

FINAL RATING

APPEARANCE ☆☆☆☆☆

TASTE ☆☆☆☆☆

MOUTHFEEL ☆☆☆☆☆

OVERALL RATING ☆☆☆☆☆

NAME	
DISTILLERY	TYPE
ORIGIN	AGE
PRICE	SAMPLED

COLOR METER

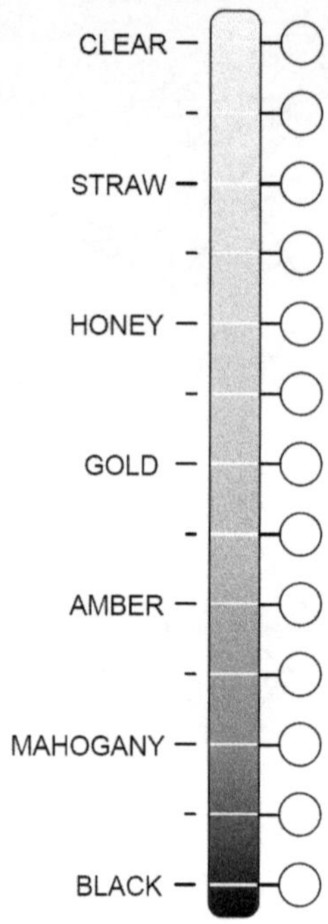

FLAVOR WHEEL

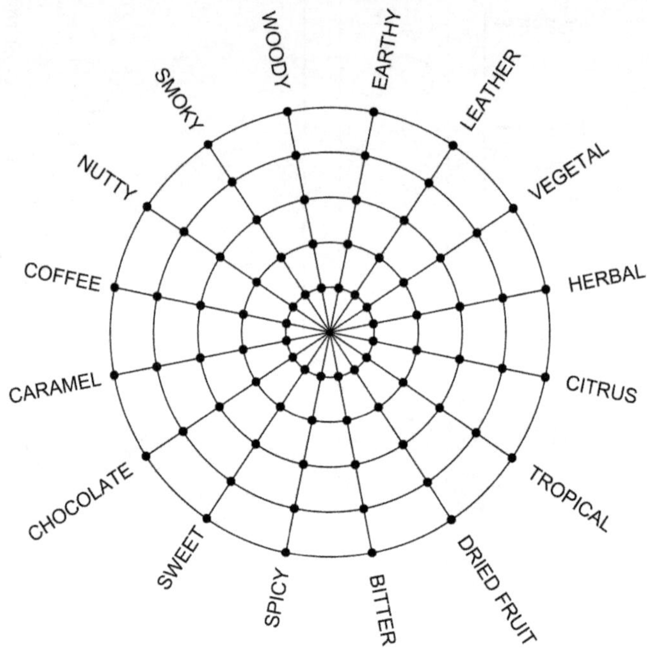

ADDITIONAL NOTES

FINAL RATING

APPEARANCE	☆☆☆☆☆
TASTE	☆☆☆☆☆
MOUTHFEEL	☆☆☆☆☆
OVERALL RATING	☆☆☆☆☆

NAME	
DISTILLERY	TYPE
ORIGIN	AGE
PRICE	SAMPLED

COLOR METER

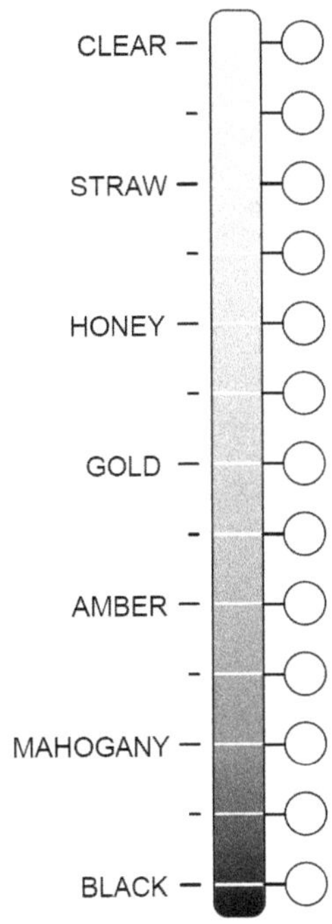

FLAVOR WHEEL

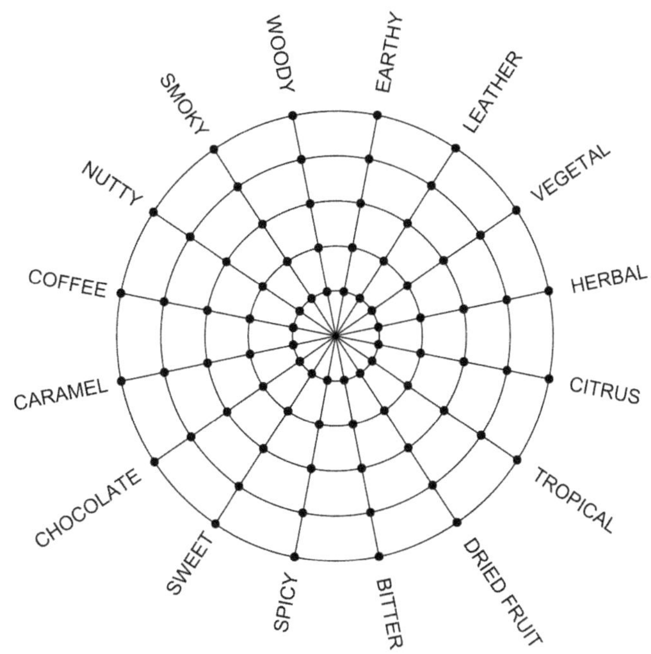

ADDITIONAL NOTES

FINAL RATING

APPEARANCE	☆☆☆☆☆
TASTE	☆☆☆☆☆
MOUTHFEEL	☆☆☆☆☆
OVERALL RATING	☆☆☆☆☆

NAME

DISTILLERY	TYPE
ORIGIN	AGE
PRICE	SAMPLED

COLOR METER

- CLEAR
- STRAW
- HONEY
- GOLD
- AMBER
- MAHOGANY
- BLACK

FLAVOR WHEEL

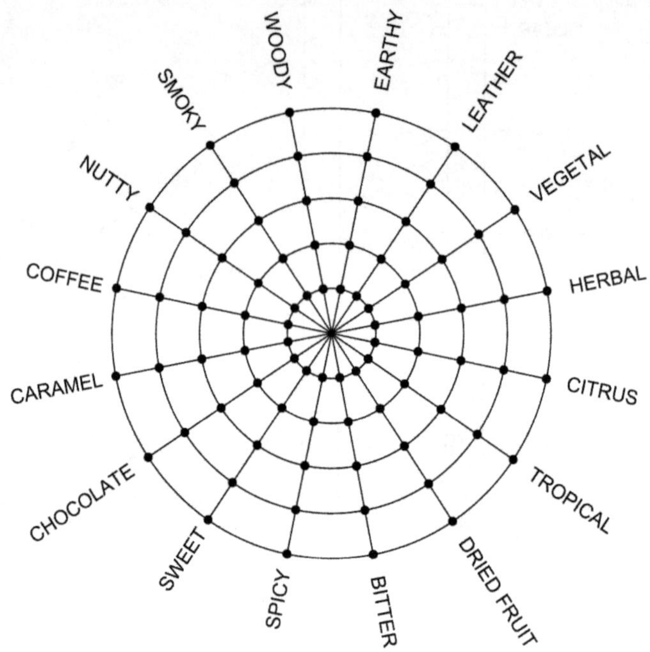

ADDITIONAL NOTES

FINAL RATING

APPEARANCE	☆☆☆☆☆
TASTE	☆☆☆☆☆
MOUTHFEEL	☆☆☆☆☆
OVERALL RATING	☆☆☆☆☆

NAME	
DISTILLERY	TYPE
ORIGIN	AGE
PRICE	SAMPLED

COLOR METER

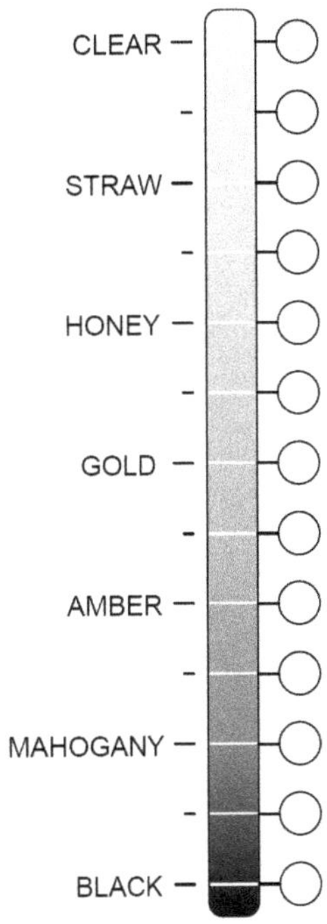

FLAVOR WHEEL

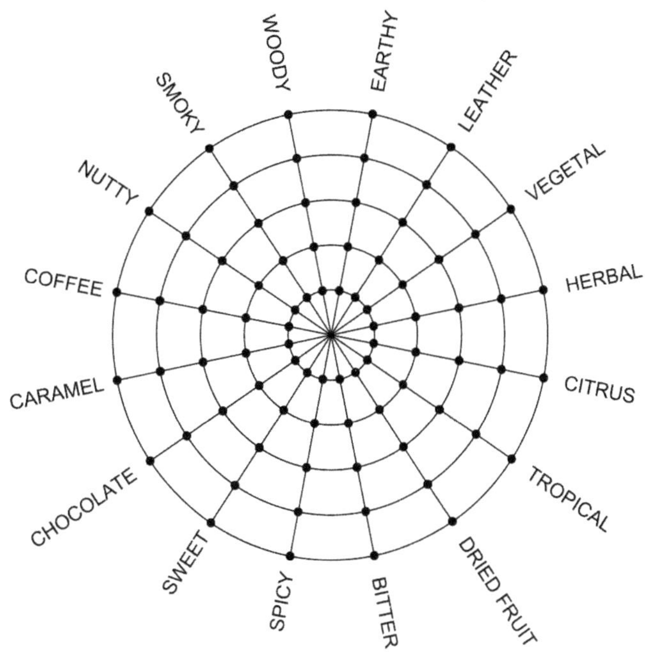

ADDITIONAL NOTES

FINAL RATING

APPEARANCE	☆☆☆☆☆
TASTE	☆☆☆☆☆
MOUTHFEEL	☆☆☆☆☆
OVERALL RATING	☆☆☆☆☆

NAME	
DISTILLERY	TYPE
ORIGIN	AGE
PRICE	SAMPLED

COLOR METER

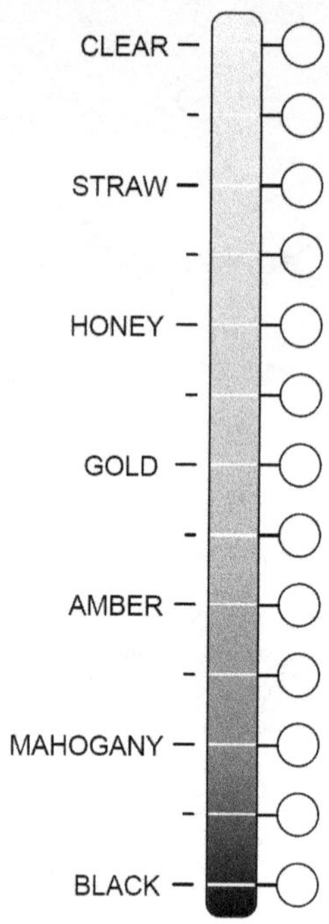

FLAVOR WHEEL

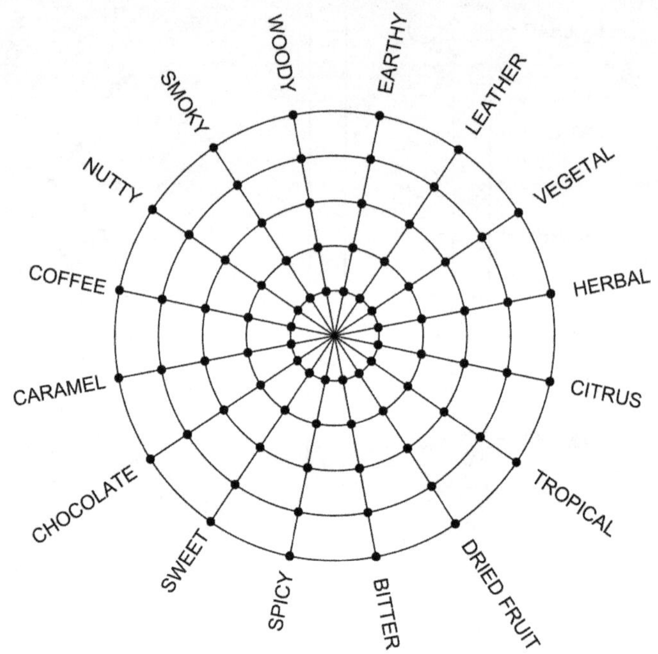

ADDITIONAL NOTES

FINAL RATING

APPEARANCE	☆☆☆☆☆
TASTE	☆☆☆☆☆
MOUTHFEEL	☆☆☆☆☆
OVERALL RATING	☆☆☆☆☆

NAME	
DISTILLERY	TYPE
ORIGIN	AGE
PRICE	SAMPLED

COLOR METER

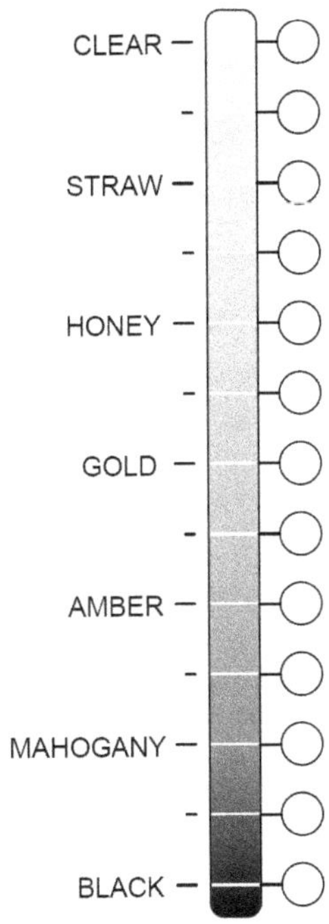

FLAVOR WHEEL

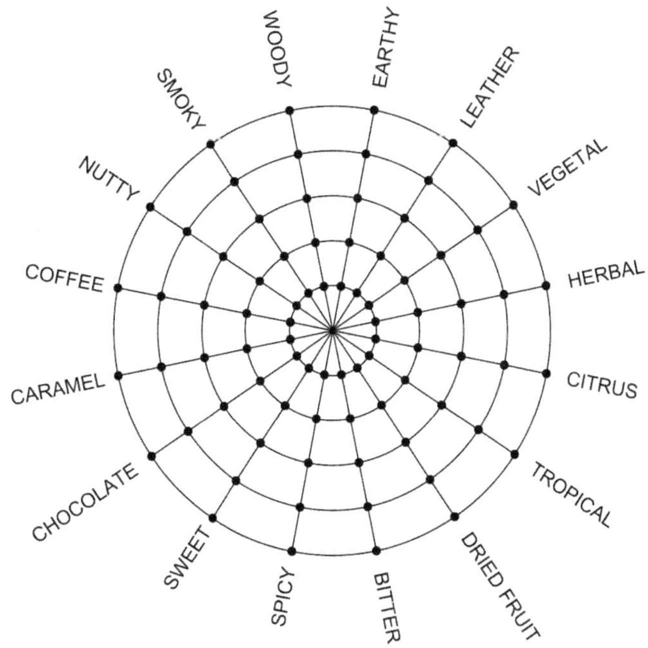

ADDITIONAL NOTES

FINAL RATING

APPEARANCE	☆☆☆☆☆
TASTE	☆☆☆☆☆
MOUTHFEEL	☆☆☆☆☆
OVERALL RATING	☆☆☆☆☆

NAME	
DISTILLERY	TYPE
ORIGIN	AGE
PRICE	SAMPLED

COLOR METER

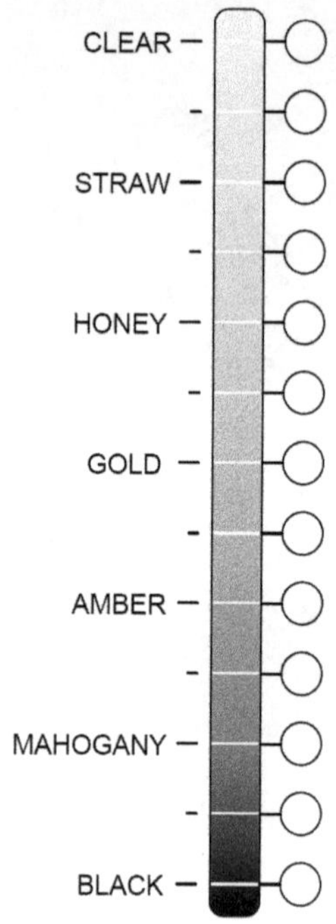

FLAVOR WHEEL

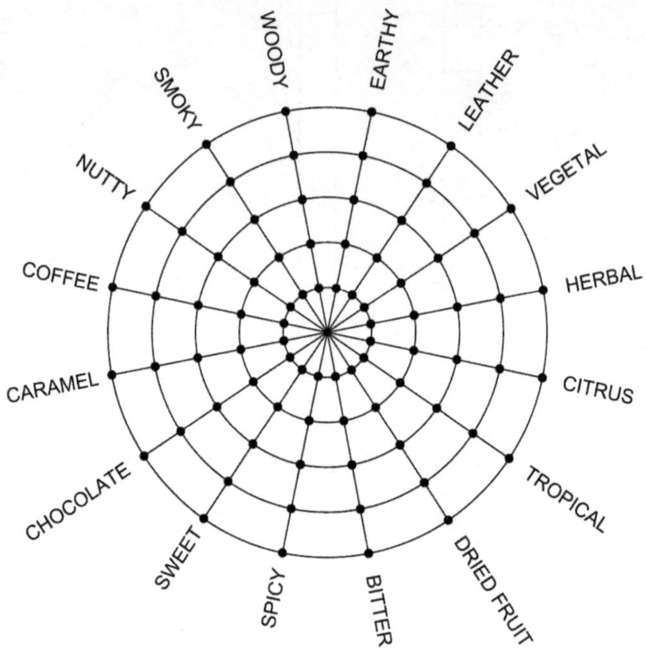

ADDITIONAL NOTES

FINAL RATING

APPEARANCE	☆☆☆☆☆
TASTE	☆☆☆☆☆
MOUTHFEEL	☆☆☆☆☆
OVERALL RATING	☆☆☆☆☆

NAME	
DISTILLERY	TYPE
ORIGIN	AGE
PRICE	SAMPLED

COLOR METER

CLEAR
STRAW
HONEY
GOLD
AMBER
MAHOGANY
BLACK

FLAVOR WHEEL

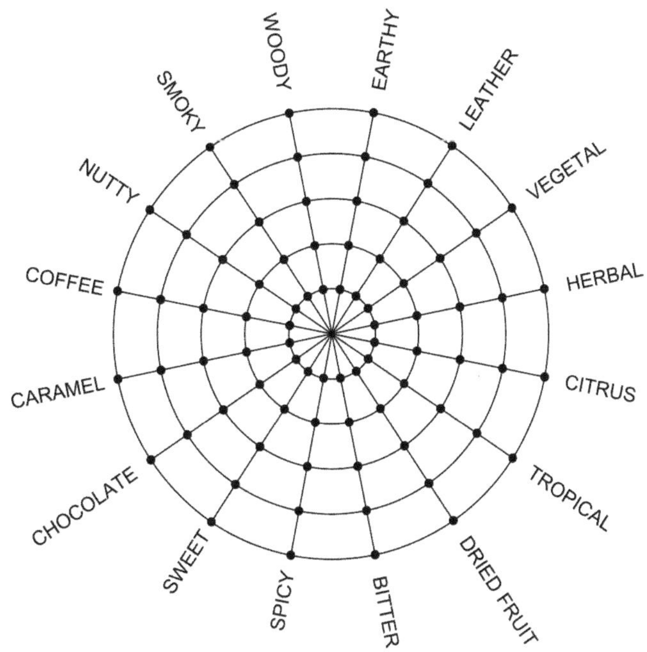

ADDITIONAL NOTES

FINAL RATING

APPEARANCE	☆☆☆☆☆
TASTE	☆☆☆☆☆
MOUTHFEEL	☆☆☆☆☆
OVERALL RATING	☆☆☆☆☆

NAME	
DISTILLERY	TYPE
ORIGIN	AGE
PRICE	SAMPLED

COLOR METER

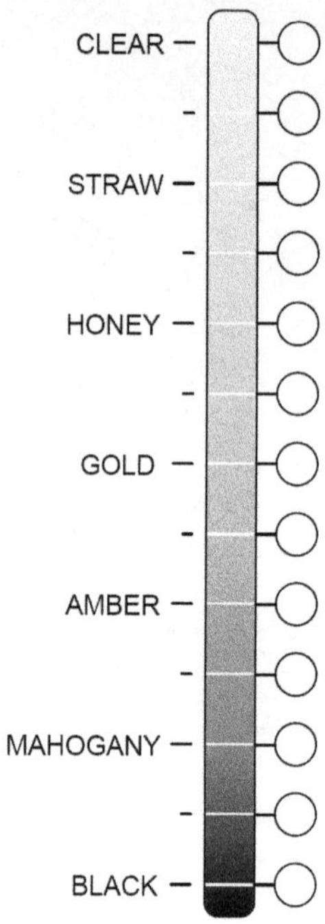

FLAVOR WHEEL

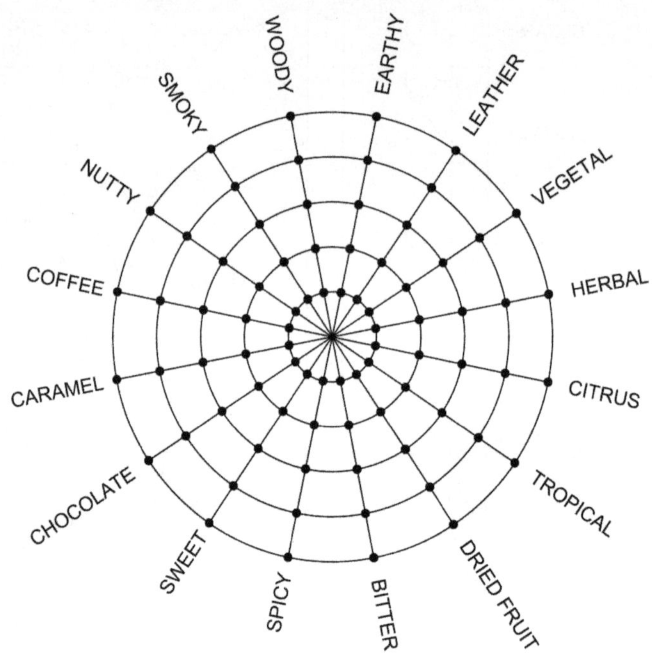

ADDITIONAL NOTES

FINAL RATING

APPEARANCE	☆☆☆☆☆
TASTE	☆☆☆☆☆
MOUTHFEEL	☆☆☆☆☆
OVERALL RATING	☆☆☆☆☆

NAME	
DISTILLERY	TYPE
ORIGIN	AGE
PRICE	SAMPLED

COLOR METER

- CLEAR
- STRAW
- HONEY
- GOLD
- AMBER
- MAHOGANY
- BLACK

FLAVOR WHEEL

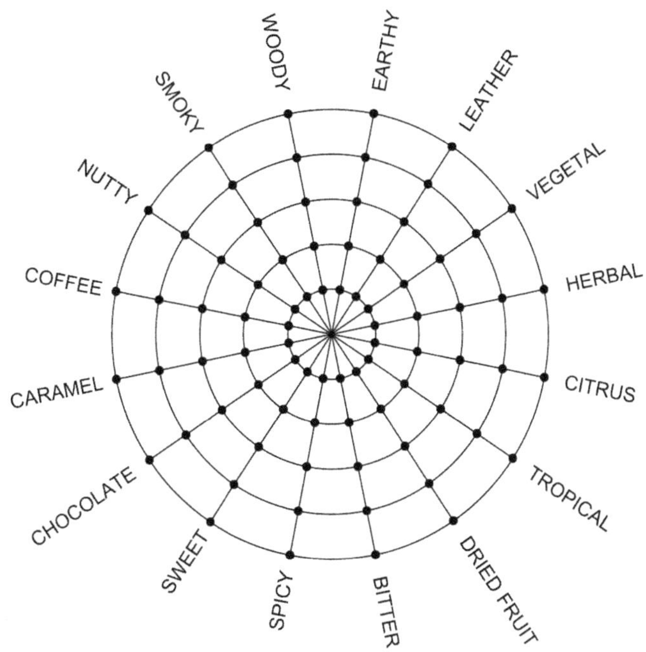

ADDITIONAL NOTES

FINAL RATING

APPEARANCE	☆☆☆☆☆
TASTE	☆☆☆☆☆
MOUTHFEEL	☆☆☆☆☆
OVERALL RATING	☆☆☆☆☆

NAME	
DISTILLERY	TYPE
ORIGIN	AGE
PRICE	SAMPLED

COLOR METER

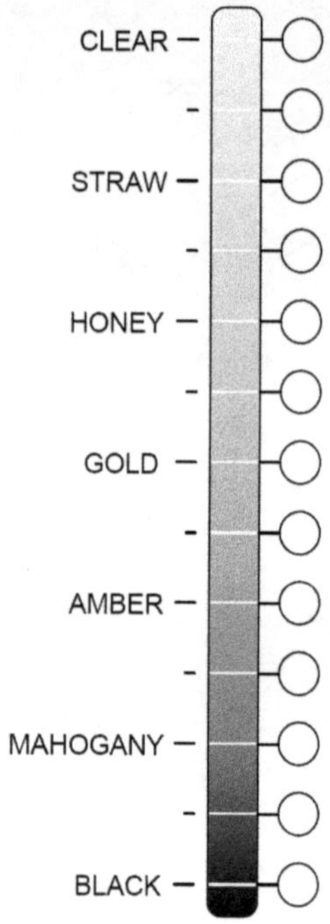

FLAVOR WHEEL

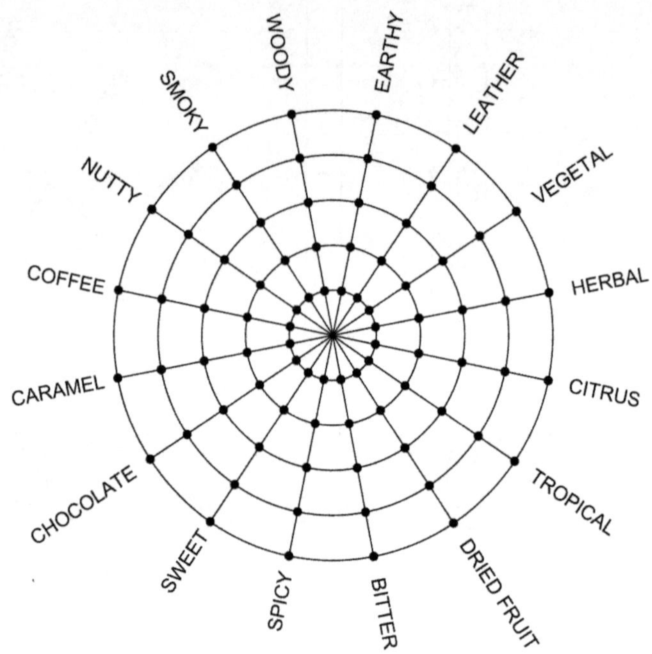

ADDITIONAL NOTES

FINAL RATING

APPEARANCE	☆☆☆☆☆
TASTE	☆☆☆☆☆
MOUTHFEEL	☆☆☆☆☆
OVERALL RATING	☆☆☆☆☆

NAME	
DISTILLERY	TYPE
ORIGIN	AGE
PRICE	SAMPLED

COLOR METER

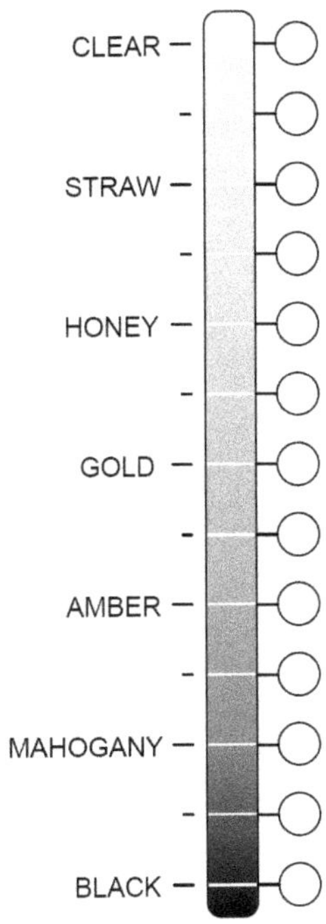

FLAVOR WHEEL

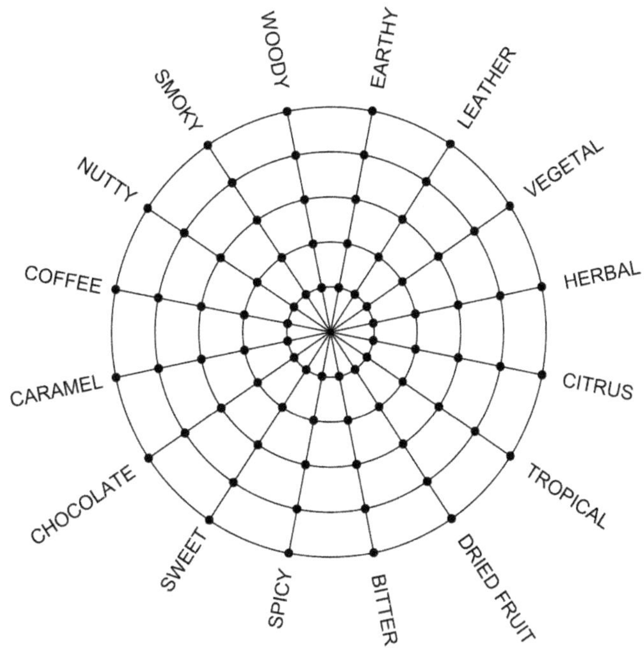

ADDITIONAL NOTES

FINAL RATING

APPEARANCE ☆☆☆☆☆

TASTE ☆☆☆☆☆

MOUTHFEEL ☆☆☆☆☆

OVERALL RATING ☆☆☆☆☆

NAME	
DISTILLERY	TYPE
ORIGIN	AGE
PRICE	SAMPLED

COLOR METER

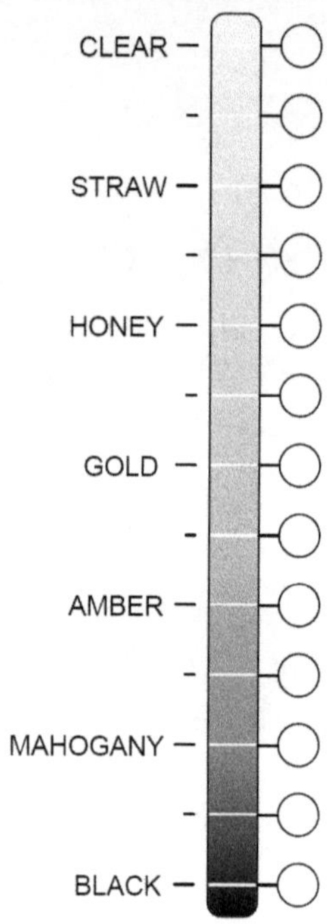

FLAVOR WHEEL

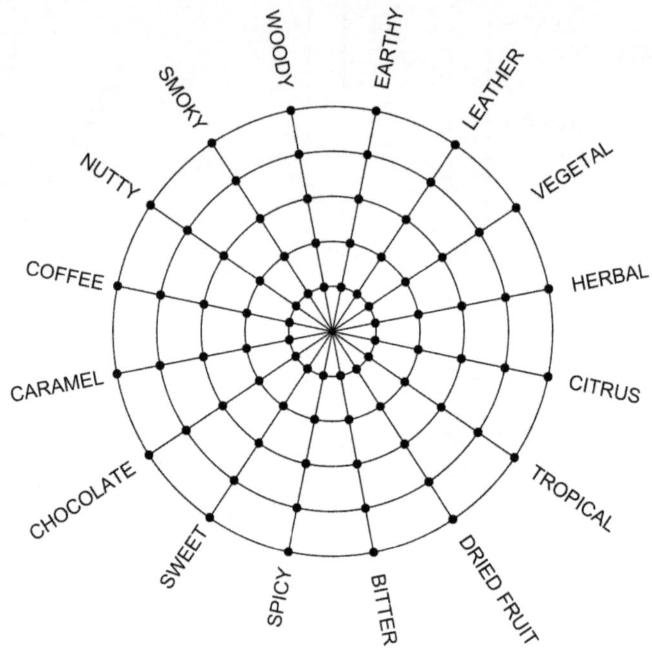

ADDITIONAL NOTES

FINAL RATING

APPEARANCE ☆☆☆☆☆

TASTE ☆☆☆☆☆

MOUTHFEEL ☆☆☆☆☆

OVERALL RATING ☆☆☆☆☆

NAME	
DISTILLERY	TYPE
ORIGIN	AGE
PRICE	SAMPLED

COLOR METER

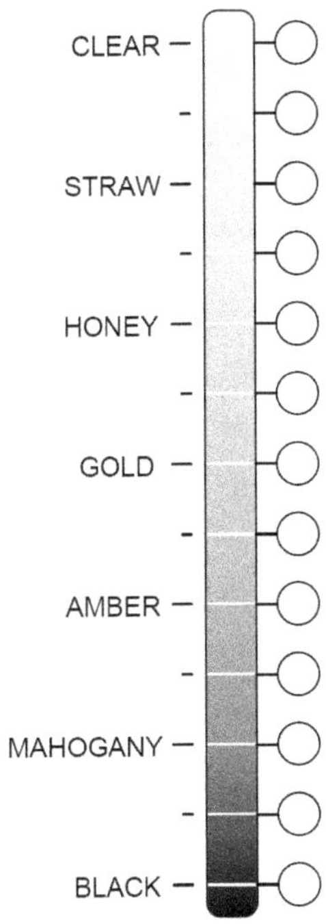

FLAVOR WHEEL

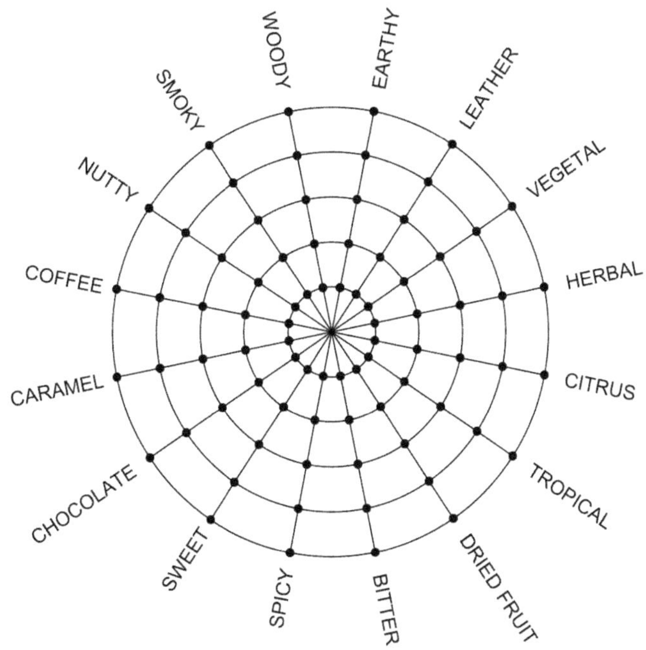

ADDITIONAL NOTES

FINAL RATING

APPEARANCE	☆☆☆☆☆
TASTE	☆☆☆☆☆
MOUTHFEEL	☆☆☆☆☆
OVERALL RATING	☆☆☆☆☆

NAME	
DISTILLERY	TYPE
ORIGIN	AGE
PRICE	SAMPLED

COLOR METER

- CLEAR
- STRAW
- HONEY
- GOLD
- AMBER
- MAHOGANY
- BLACK

FLAVOR WHEEL

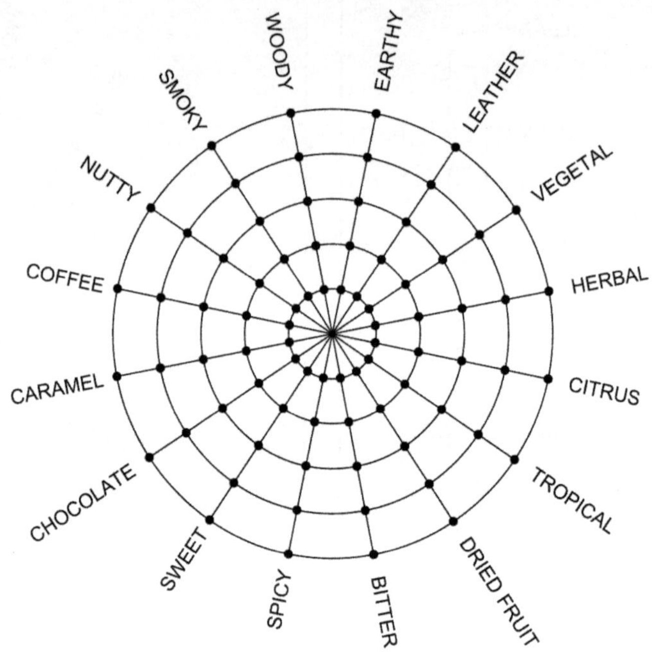

ADDITIONAL NOTES

FINAL RATING

APPEARANCE	☆☆☆☆☆
TASTE	☆☆☆☆☆
MOUTHFEEL	☆☆☆☆☆
OVERALL RATING	☆☆☆☆☆

NAME

DISTILLERY	TYPE
ORIGIN	AGE
PRICE	SAMPLED

COLOR METER

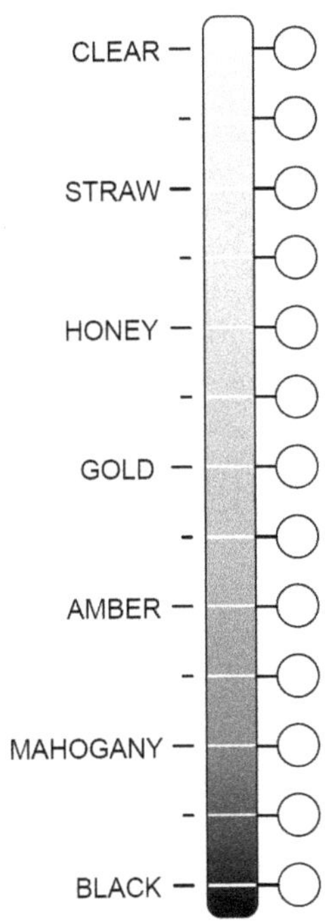

FLAVOR WHEEL

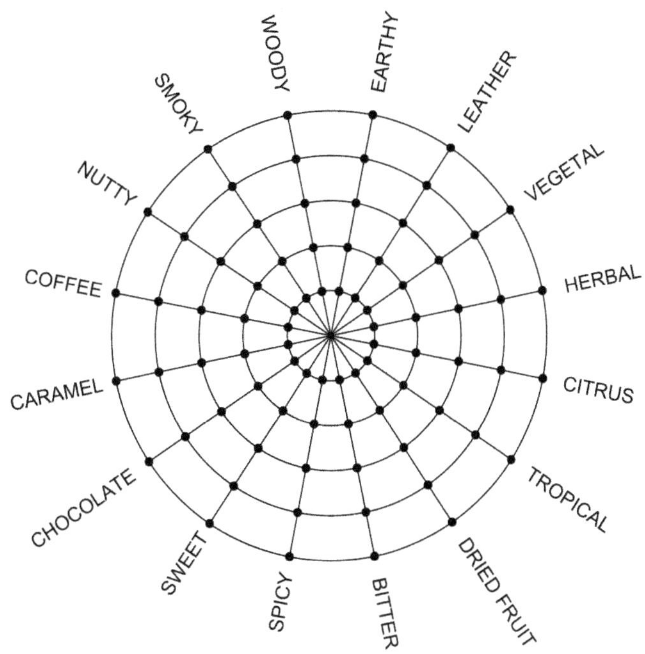

ADDITIONAL NOTES

FINAL RATING

APPEARANCE	☆☆☆☆☆
TASTE	☆☆☆☆☆
MOUTHFEEL	☆☆☆☆☆
OVERALL RATING	☆☆☆☆☆

NAME	
DISTILLERY	TYPE
ORIGIN	AGE
PRICE	SAMPLED

COLOR METER

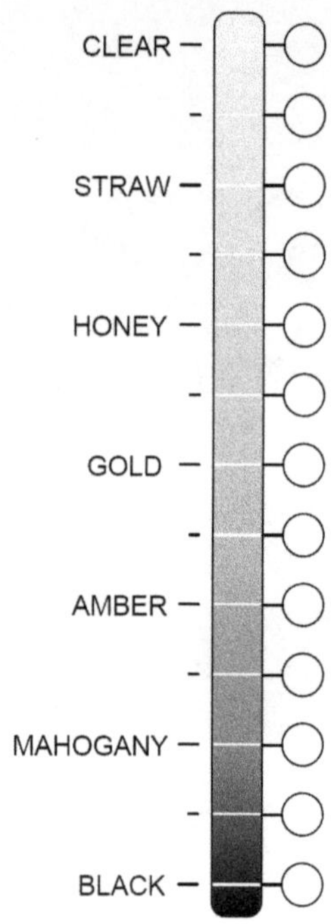

FLAVOR WHEEL

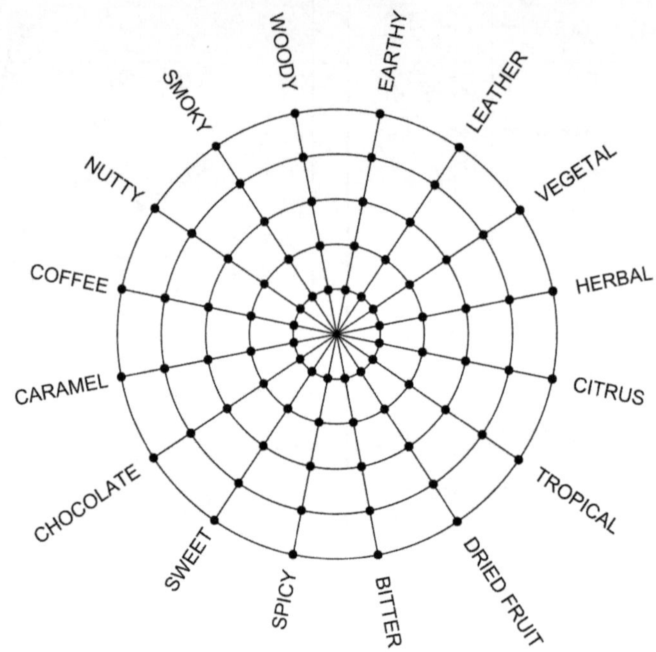

ADDITIONAL NOTES

FINAL RATING

APPEARANCE ☆☆☆☆☆

TASTE ☆☆☆☆☆

MOUTHFEEL ☆☆☆☆☆

OVERALL RATING ☆☆☆☆☆

NAME	
DISTILLERY	TYPE
ORIGIN	AGE
PRICE	SAMPLED

COLOR METER

- CLEAR
- STRAW
- HONEY
- GOLD
- AMBER
- MAHOGANY
- BLACK

FLAVOR WHEEL

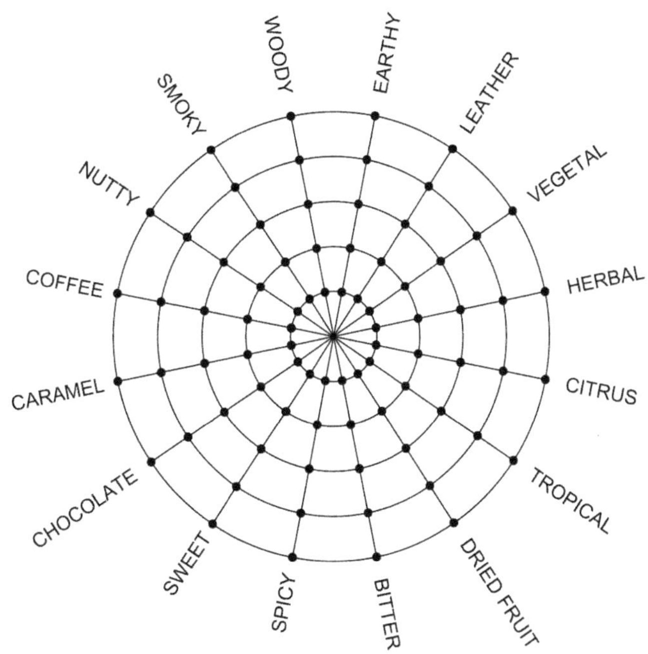

ADDITIONAL NOTES

FINAL RATING

APPEARANCE	☆☆☆☆☆
TASTE	☆☆☆☆☆
MOUTHFEEL	☆☆☆☆☆
OVERALL RATING	☆☆☆☆☆

NAME	
DISTILLERY	TYPE
ORIGIN	AGE
PRICE	SAMPLED

COLOR METER

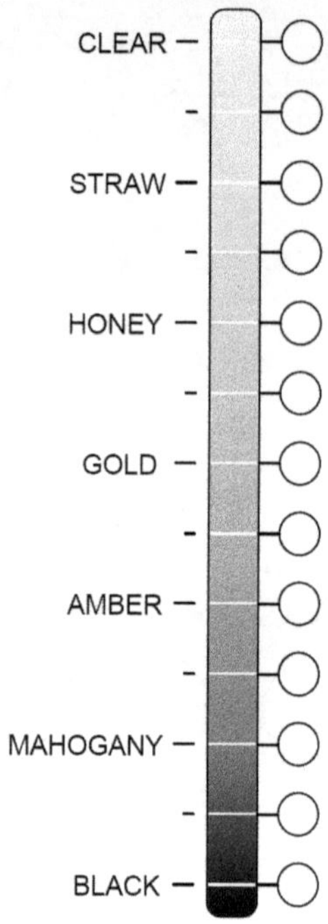

FLAVOR WHEEL

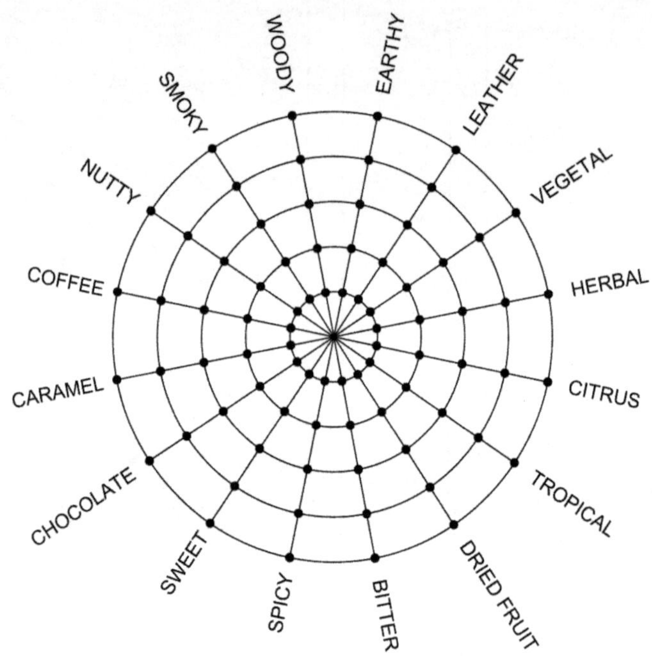

ADDITIONAL NOTES

FINAL RATING

APPEARANCE	☆☆☆☆☆
TASTE	☆☆☆☆☆
MOUTHFEEL	☆☆☆☆☆
OVERALL RATING	☆☆☆☆☆

NAME

DISTILLERY	TYPE
ORIGIN	AGE
PRICE	SAMPLED

COLOR METER

- CLEAR
- STRAW
- HONEY
- GOLD
- AMBER
- MAHOGANY
- BLACK

FLAVOR WHEEL

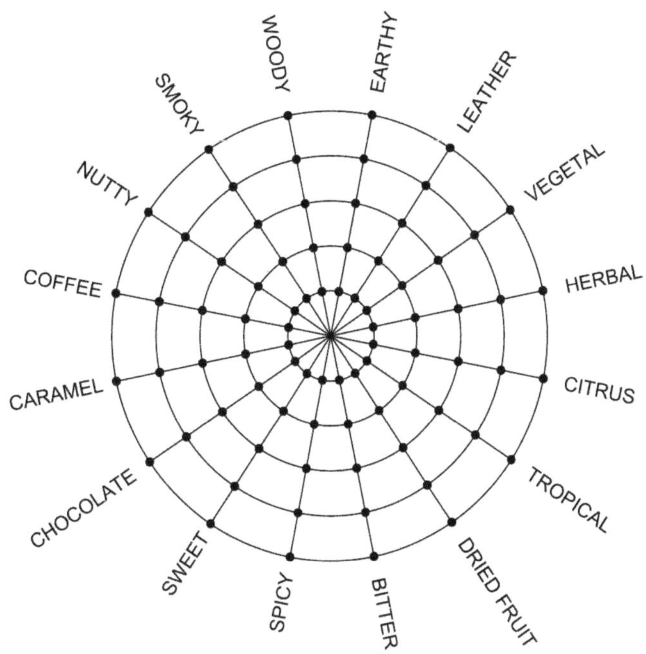

ADDITIONAL NOTES

FINAL RATING

APPEARANCE	☆☆☆☆☆
TASTE	☆☆☆☆☆
MOUTHFEEL	☆☆☆☆☆
OVERALL RATING	☆☆☆☆☆

NAME	
DISTILLERY	TYPE
ORIGIN	AGE
PRICE	SAMPLED

COLOR METER

- CLEAR
- -
- STRAW
- -
- HONEY
- -
- GOLD
- -
- AMBER
- -
- MAHOGANY
- -
- BLACK

FLAVOR WHEEL

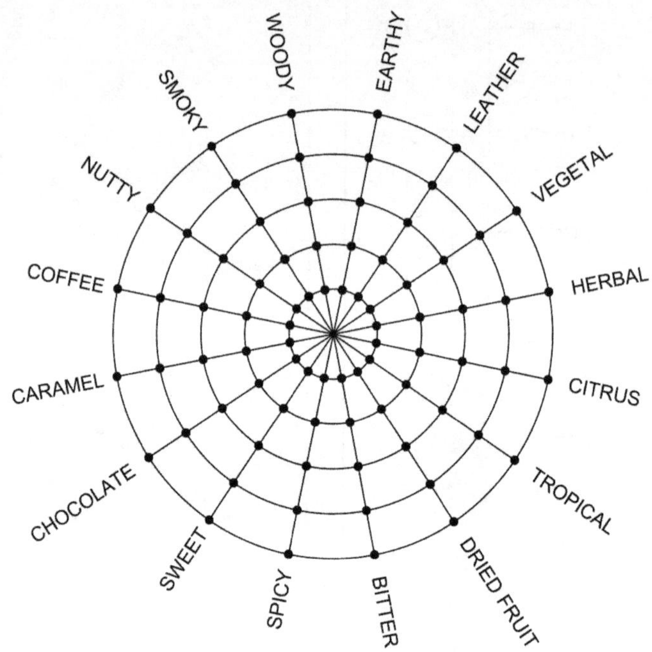

ADDITIONAL NOTES

FINAL RATING

APPEARANCE	☆☆☆☆☆
TASTE	☆☆☆☆☆
MOUTHFEEL	☆☆☆☆☆
OVERALL RATING	☆☆☆☆☆

NAME	
DISTILLERY	TYPE
ORIGIN	AGE
PRICE	SAMPLED

COLOR METER

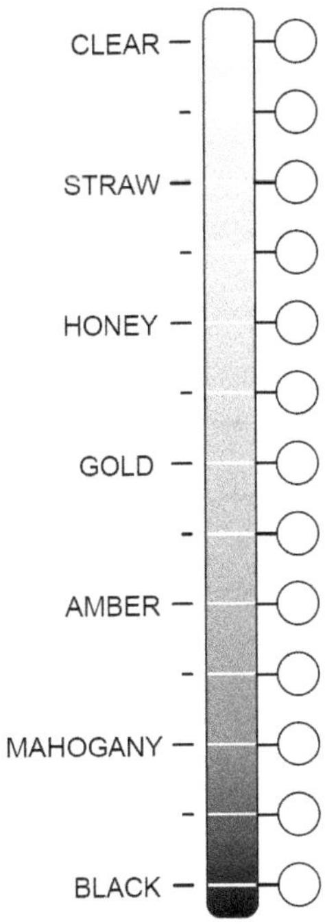

FLAVOR WHEEL

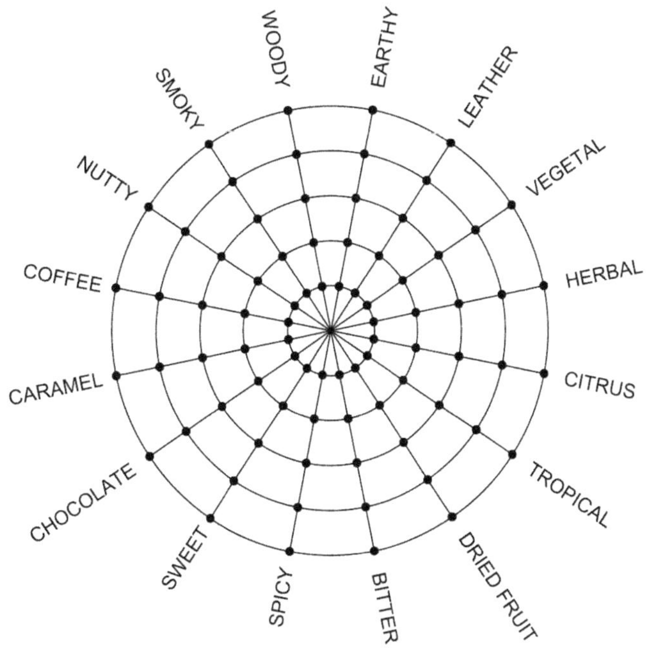

ADDITIONAL NOTES

FINAL RATING

APPEARANCE	☆☆☆☆☆
TASTE	☆☆☆☆☆
MOUTHFEEL	☆☆☆☆☆
OVERALL RATING	☆☆☆☆☆

NAME	
DISTILLERY	TYPE
ORIGIN	AGE
PRICE	SAMPLED

COLOR METER

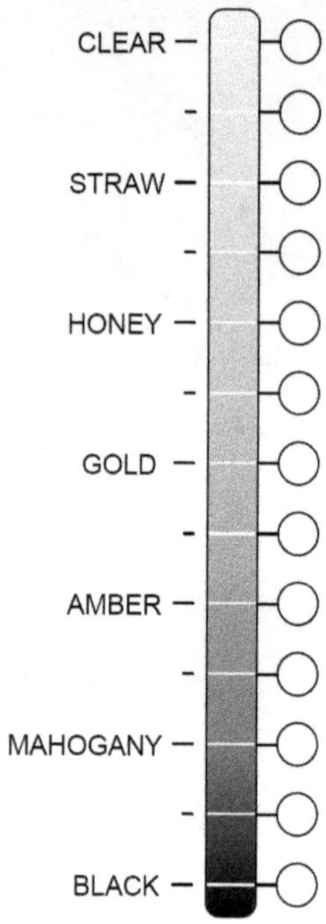

FLAVOR WHEEL

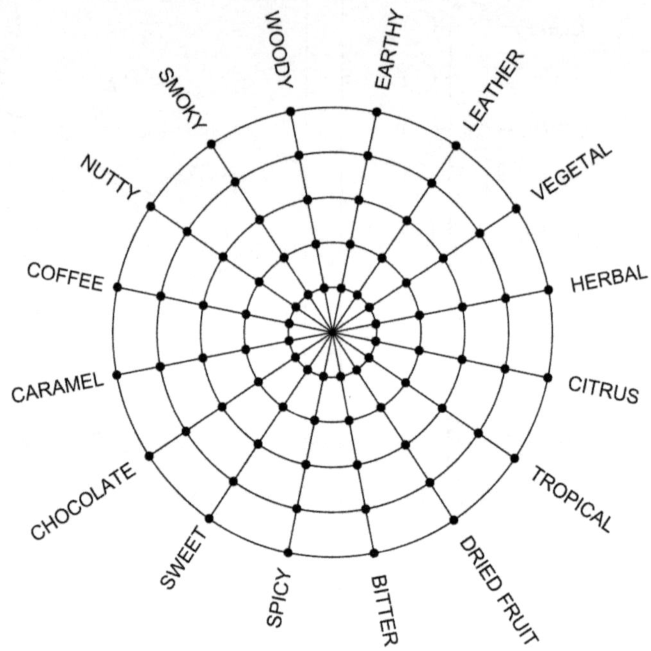

ADDITIONAL NOTES

FINAL RATING

APPEARANCE	☆☆☆☆☆
TASTE	☆☆☆☆☆
MOUTHFEEL	☆☆☆☆☆
OVERALL RATING	☆☆☆☆☆

NAME	
DISTILLERY	TYPE
ORIGIN	AGE
PRICE	SAMPLED

COLOR METER

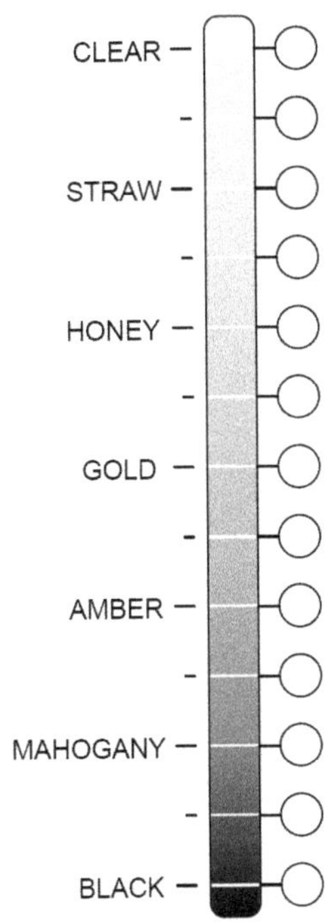

FLAVOR WHEEL

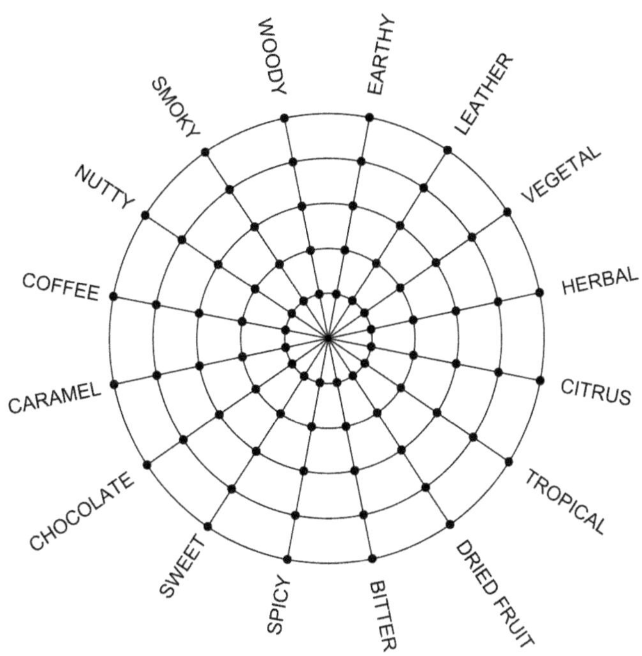

ADDITIONAL NOTES

FINAL RATING

APPEARANCE	☆☆☆☆☆
TASTE	☆☆☆☆☆
MOUTHFEEL	☆☆☆☆☆
OVERALL RATING	☆☆☆☆☆

NAME	
DISTILLERY	TYPE
ORIGIN	AGE
PRICE	SAMPLED

COLOR METER

- CLEAR
- STRAW
- HONEY
- GOLD
- AMBER
- MAHOGANY
- BLACK

FLAVOR WHEEL

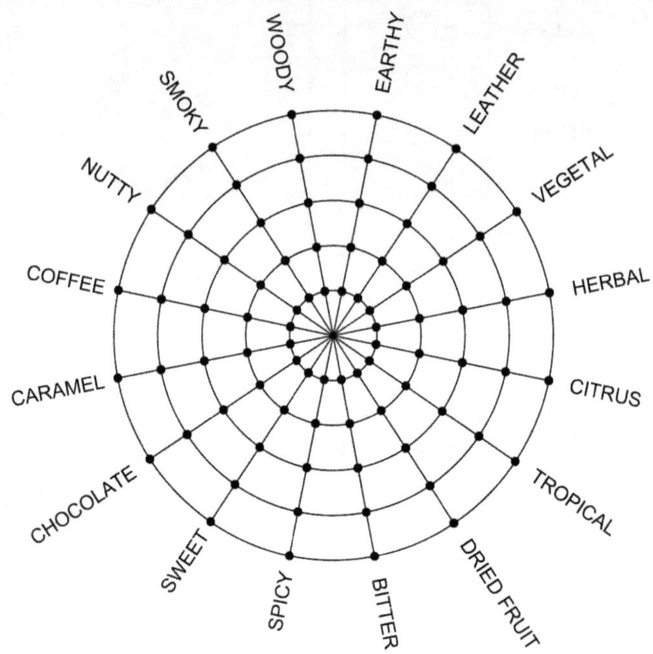

ADDITIONAL NOTES

FINAL RATING

APPEARANCE	☆☆☆☆☆
TASTE	☆☆☆☆☆
MOUTHFEEL	☆☆☆☆☆
OVERALL RATING	☆☆☆☆☆

NAME	
DISTILLERY	TYPE
ORIGIN	AGE
PRICE	SAMPLED

COLOR METER

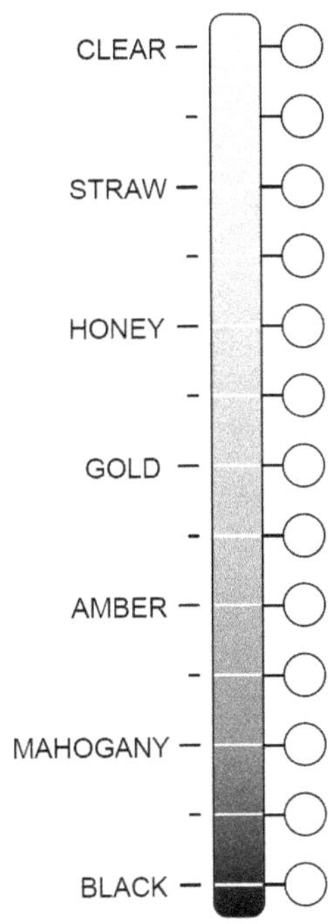

FLAVOR WHEEL

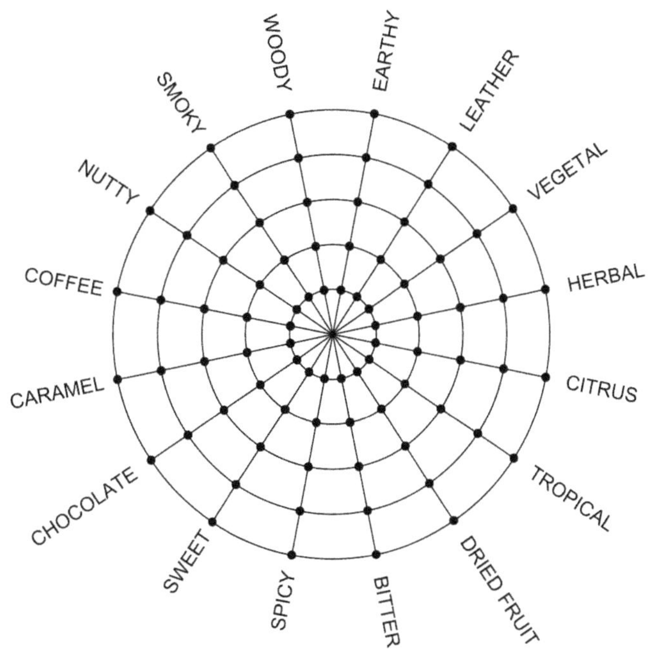

ADDITIONAL NOTES

FINAL RATING

APPEARANCE	☆☆☆☆☆
TASTE	☆☆☆☆☆
MOUTHFEEL	☆☆☆☆☆
OVERALL RATING	☆☆☆☆☆

NAME	
DISTILLERY	TYPE
ORIGIN	AGE
PRICE	SAMPLED

COLOR METER

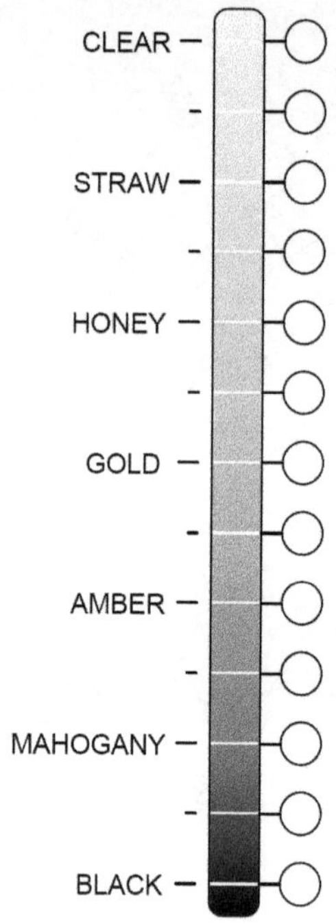

FLAVOR WHEEL

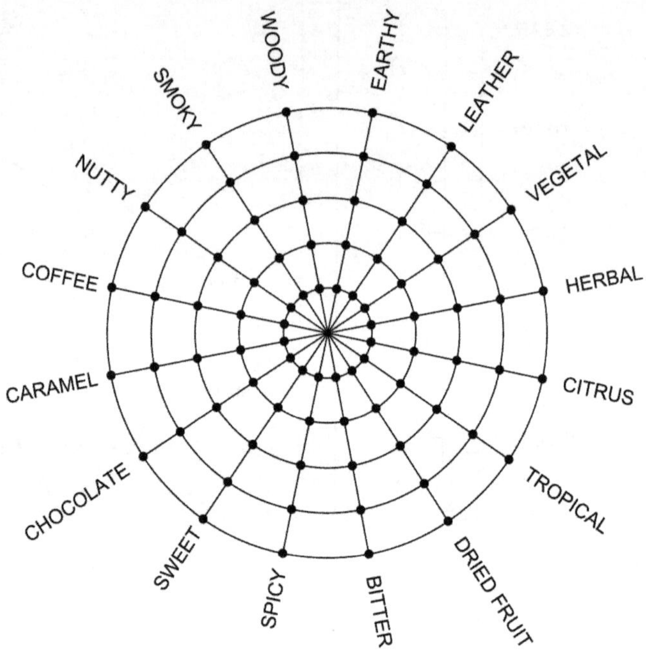

ADDITIONAL NOTES

FINAL RATING

APPEARANCE ☆☆☆☆☆

TASTE ☆☆☆☆☆

MOUTHFEEL ☆☆☆☆☆

OVERALL RATING ☆☆☆☆☆

NAME	
DISTILLERY	TYPE
ORIGIN	AGE
PRICE	SAMPLED

COLOR METER

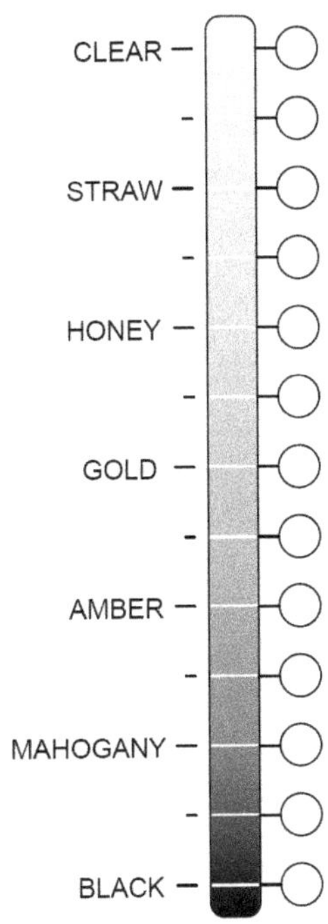

FLAVOR WHEEL

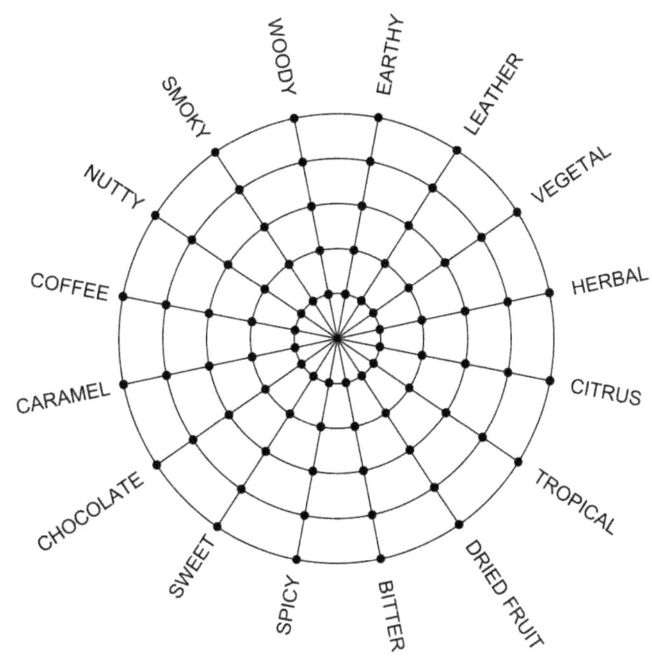

ADDITIONAL NOTES

FINAL RATING

APPEARANCE	☆☆☆☆☆
TASTE	☆☆☆☆☆
MOUTHFEEL	☆☆☆☆☆
OVERALL RATING	☆☆☆☆☆

NAME

DISTILLERY	TYPE
ORIGIN	AGE
PRICE	SAMPLED

COLOR METER

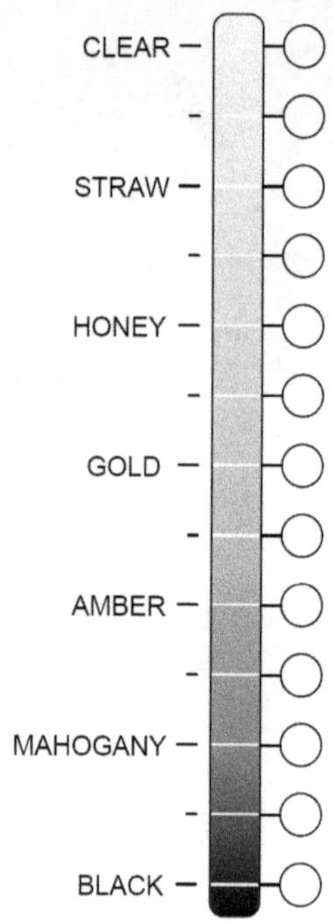

FLAVOR WHEEL

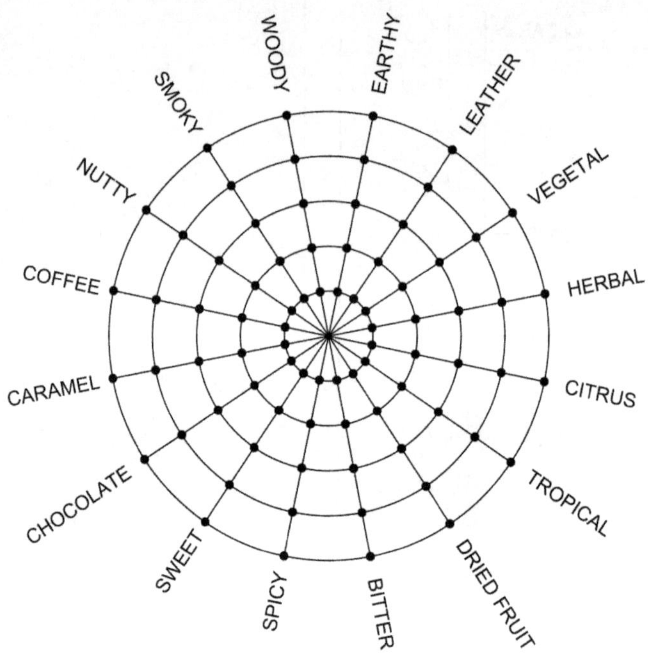

ADDITIONAL NOTES

FINAL RATING

APPEARANCE	☆☆☆☆☆
TASTE	☆☆☆☆☆
MOUTHFEEL	☆☆☆☆☆
OVERALL RATING	☆☆☆☆☆

NAME	
DISTILLERY	TYPE
ORIGIN	AGE
PRICE	SAMPLED

COLOR METER

- CLEAR
- STRAW
- HONEY
- GOLD
- AMBER
- MAHOGANY
- BLACK

FLAVOR WHEEL

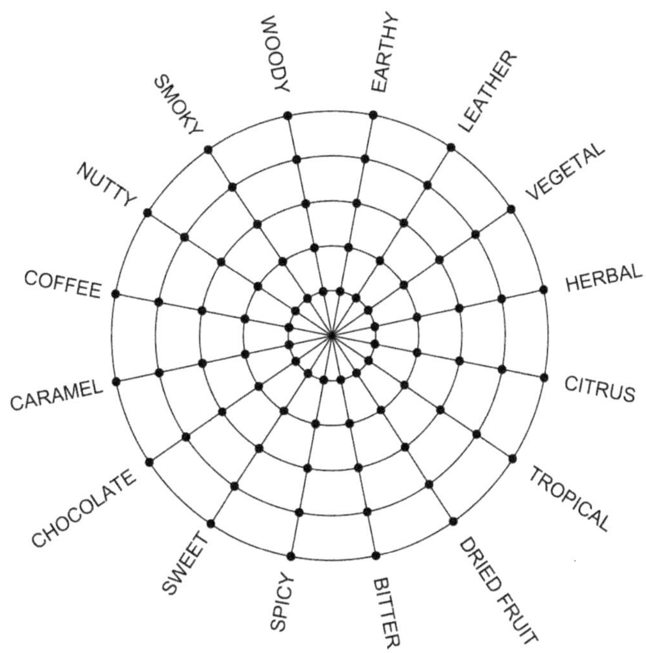

ADDITIONAL NOTES

FINAL RATING

APPEARANCE	☆☆☆☆☆
TASTE	☆☆☆☆☆
MOUTHFEEL	☆☆☆☆☆
OVERALL RATING	☆☆☆☆☆

NAME	
DISTILLERY	TYPE
ORIGIN	AGE
PRICE	SAMPLED

COLOR METER

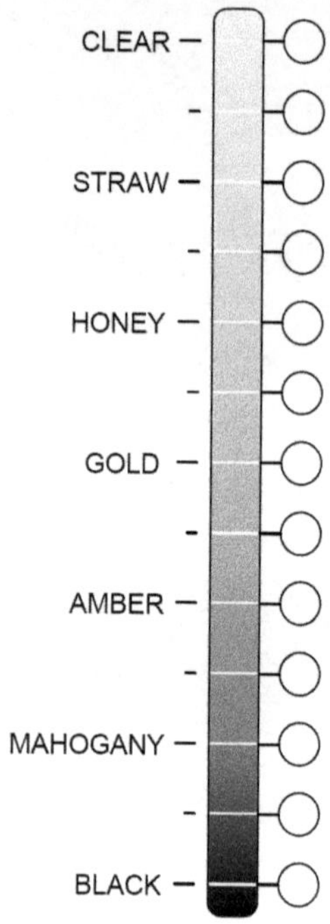

FLAVOR WHEEL

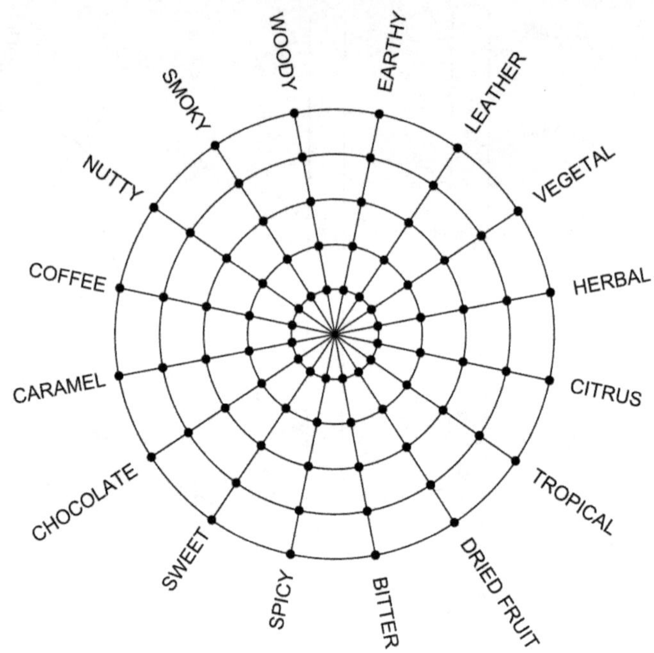

ADDITIONAL NOTES

FINAL RATING

APPEARANCE ☆☆☆☆☆

TASTE ☆☆☆☆☆

MOUTHFEEL ☆☆☆☆☆

OVERALL RATING ☆☆☆☆☆

NAME

DISTILLERY | TYPE

ORIGIN | AGE

PRICE | SAMPLED

COLOR METER

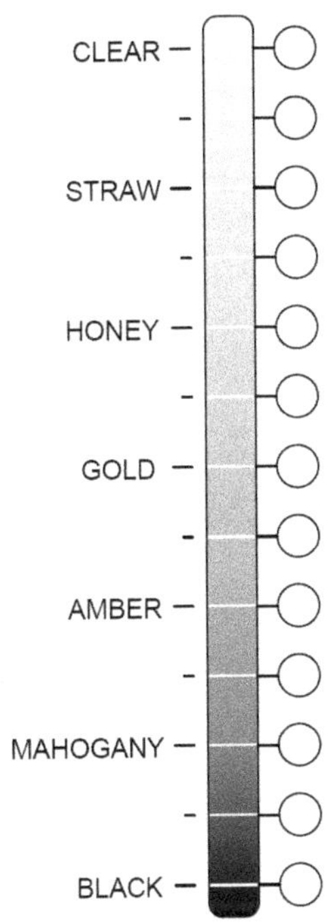

FLAVOR WHEEL

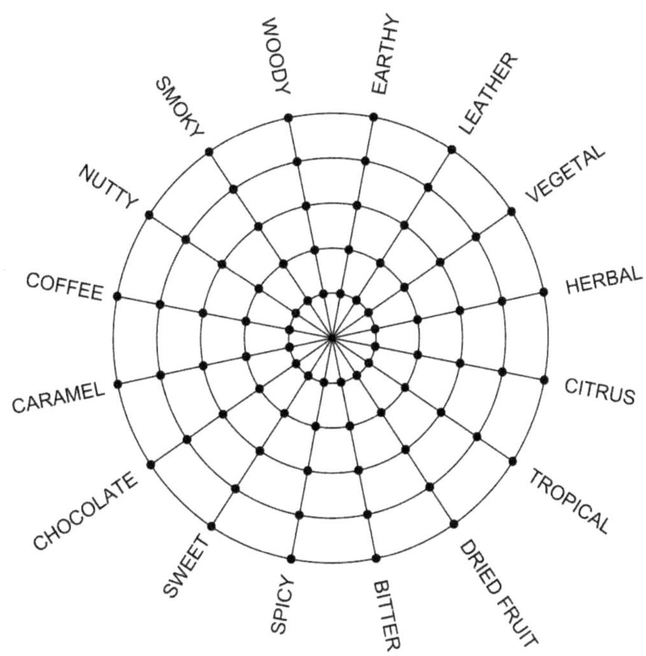

ADDITIONAL NOTES

FINAL RATING

APPEARANCE	☆☆☆☆☆
TASTE	☆☆☆☆☆
MOUTHFEEL	☆☆☆☆☆
OVERALL RATING	☆☆☆☆☆

NAME	
DISTILLERY	TYPE
ORIGIN	AGE
PRICE	SAMPLED

COLOR METER

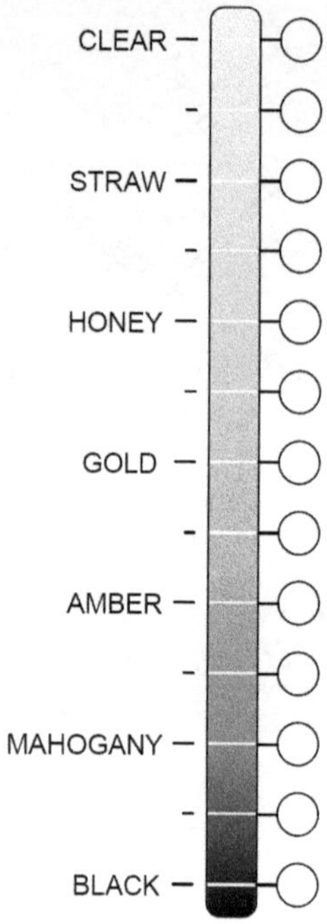

FLAVOR WHEEL

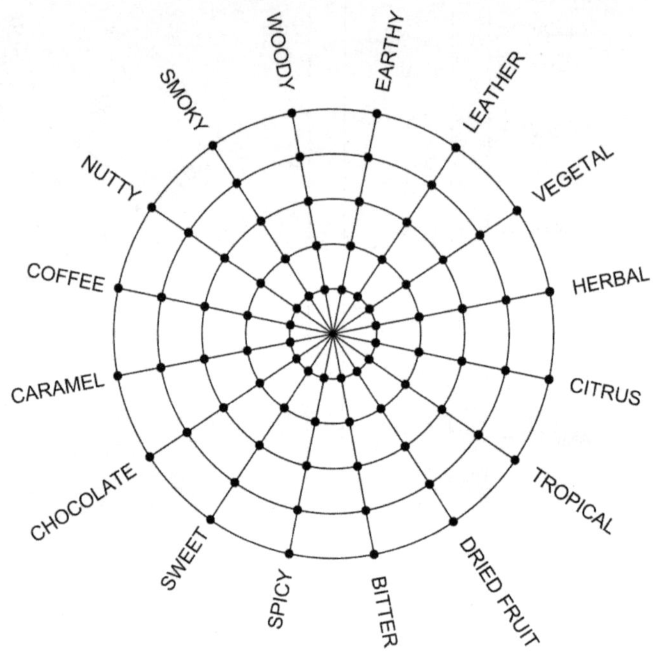

ADDITIONAL NOTES

FINAL RATING

APPEARANCE ☆☆☆☆☆

TASTE ☆☆☆☆☆

MOUTHFEEL ☆☆☆☆☆

OVERALL RATING ☆☆☆☆☆

NAME	
DISTILLERY	TYPE
ORIGIN	AGE
PRICE	SAMPLED

COLOR METER

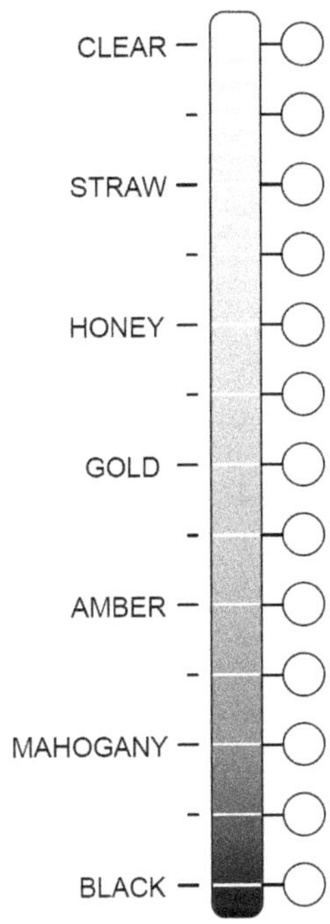

FLAVOR WHEEL

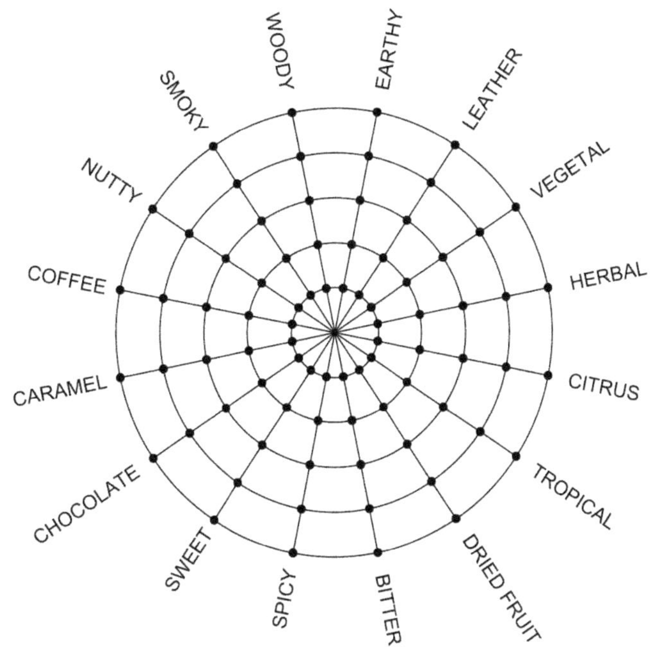

ADDITIONAL NOTES

FINAL RATING

APPEARANCE	☆☆☆☆☆
TASTE	☆☆☆☆☆
MOUTHFEEL	☆☆☆☆☆
OVERALL RATING	☆☆☆☆☆

NAME

DISTILLERY | TYPE

ORIGIN | AGE

PRICE | SAMPLED

COLOR METER

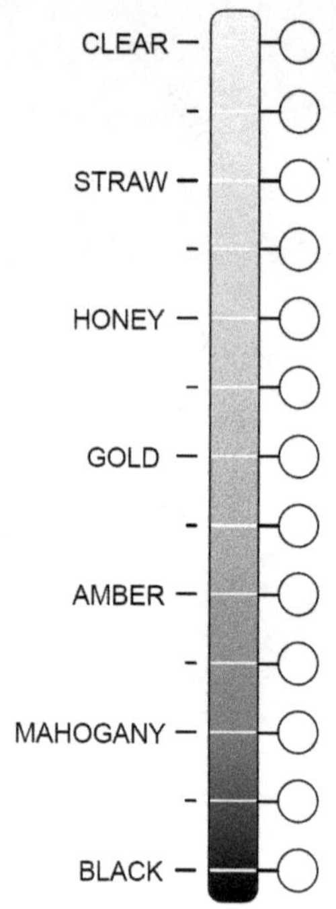

FLAVOR WHEEL

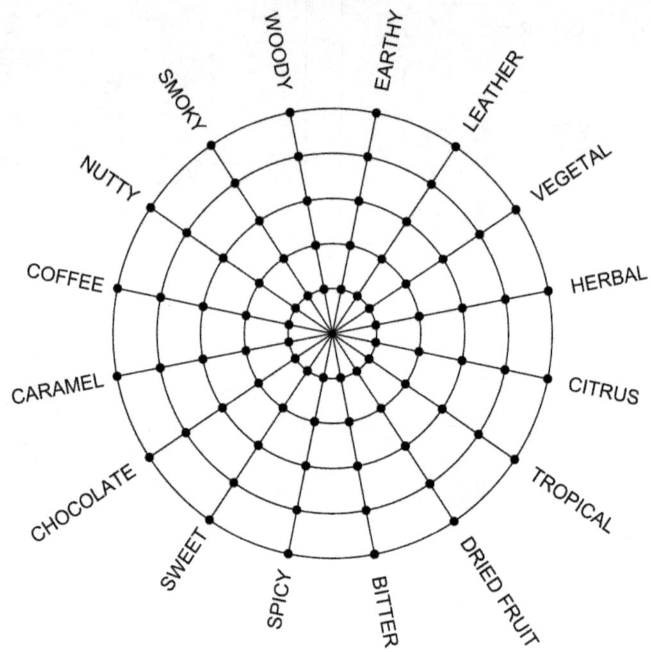

ADDITIONAL NOTES

FINAL RATING

APPEARANCE ☆☆☆☆☆

TASTE ☆☆☆☆☆

MOUTHFEEL ☆☆☆☆☆

OVERALL RATING ☆☆☆☆☆

NAME	
DISTILLERY	TYPE
ORIGIN	AGE
PRICE	SAMPLED

COLOR METER

- CLEAR
- STRAW
- HONEY
- GOLD
- AMBER
- MAHOGANY
- BLACK

FLAVOR WHEEL

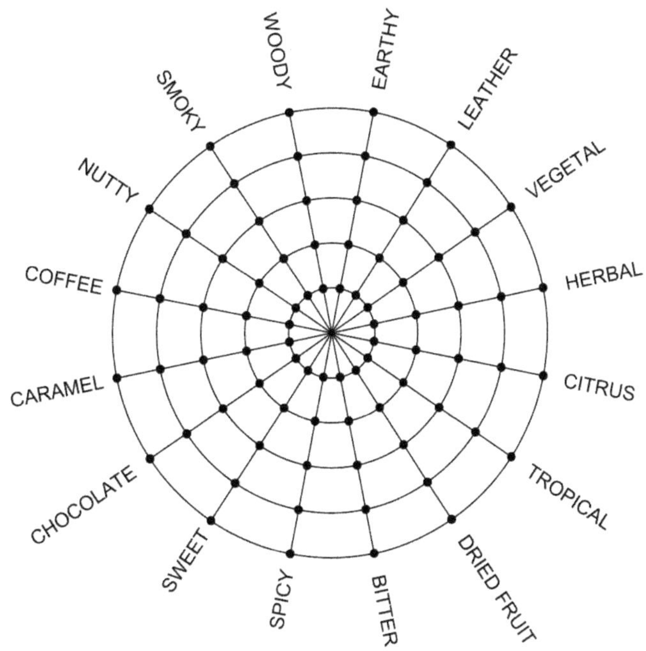

ADDITIONAL NOTES

FINAL RATING

APPEARANCE	☆☆☆☆☆
TASTE	☆☆☆☆☆
MOUTHFEEL	☆☆☆☆☆
OVERALL RATING	☆☆☆☆☆

NAME	
DISTILLERY	TYPE
ORIGIN	AGE
PRICE	SAMPLED

COLOR METER

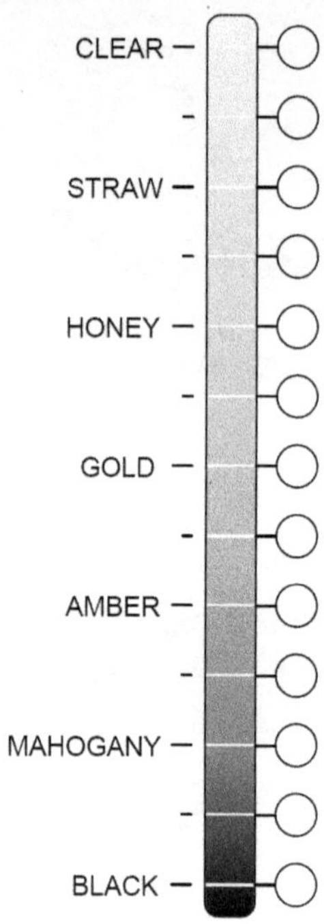

FLAVOR WHEEL

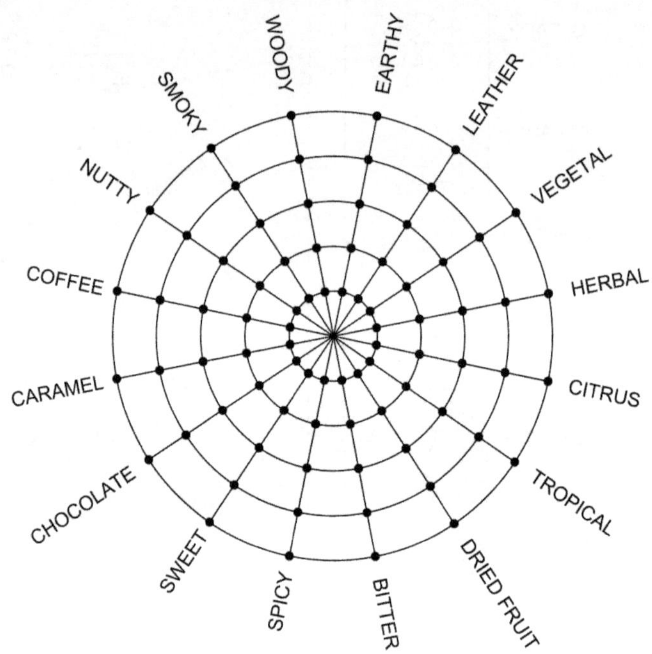

ADDITIONAL NOTES

FINAL RATING

APPEARANCE	☆☆☆☆☆
TASTE	☆☆☆☆☆
MOUTHFEEL	☆☆☆☆☆
OVERALL RATING	☆☆☆☆☆

NAME

DISTILLERY | TYPE

ORIGIN | AGE

PRICE | SAMPLED

COLOR METER

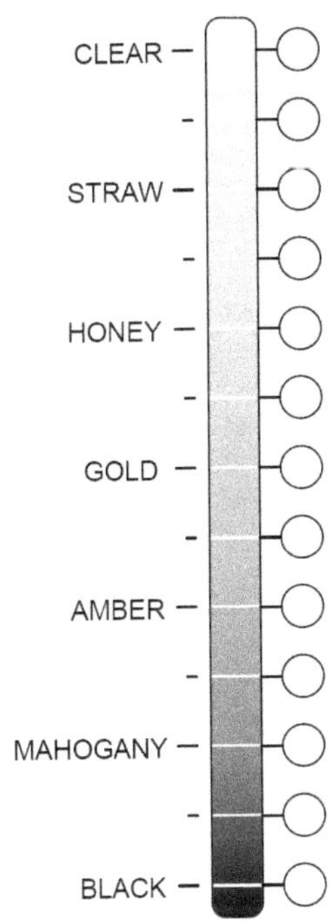

FLAVOR WHEEL

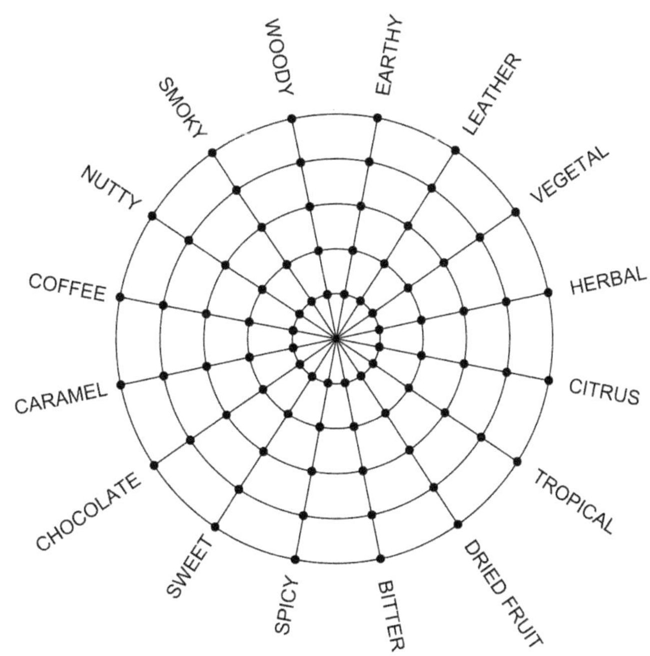

ADDITIONAL NOTES

FINAL RATING

APPEARANCE ☆☆☆☆☆

TASTE ☆☆☆☆☆

MOUTHFEEL ☆☆☆☆☆

OVERALL RATING ☆☆☆☆☆

NAME	
DISTILLERY	TYPE
ORIGIN	AGE
PRICE	SAMPLED

COLOR METER

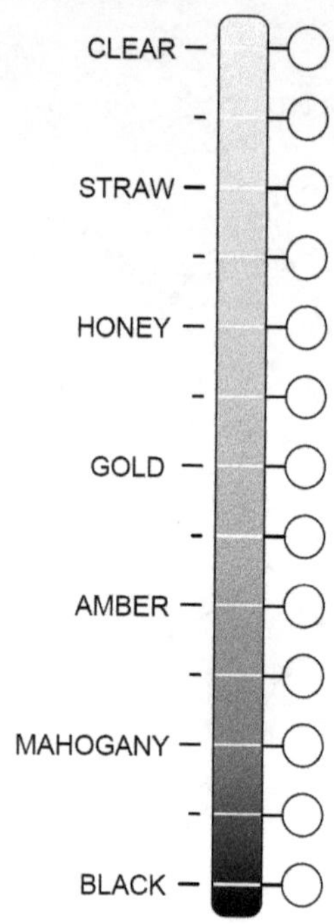

FLAVOR WHEEL

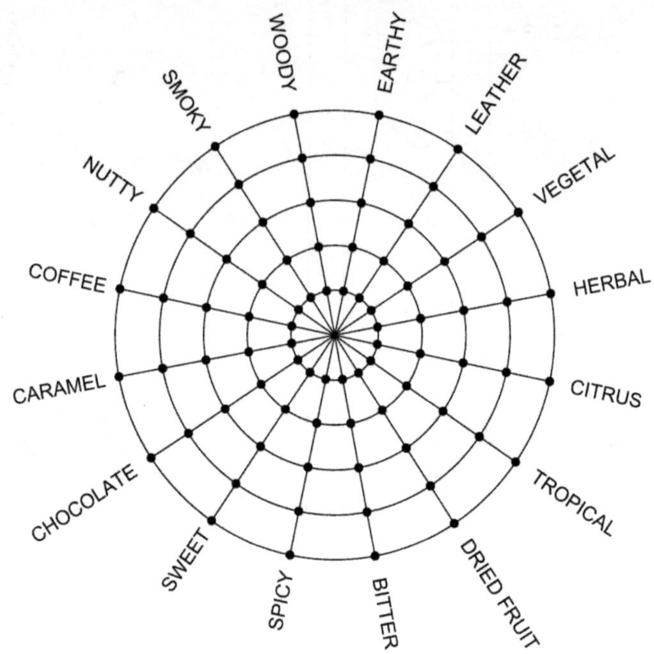

ADDITIONAL NOTES

FINAL RATING

APPEARANCE	☆☆☆☆☆
TASTE	☆☆☆☆☆
MOUTHFEEL	☆☆☆☆☆
OVERALL RATING	☆☆☆☆☆

NAME

DISTILLERY

TYPE

ORIGIN

AGE

PRICE

SAMPLED

COLOR METER

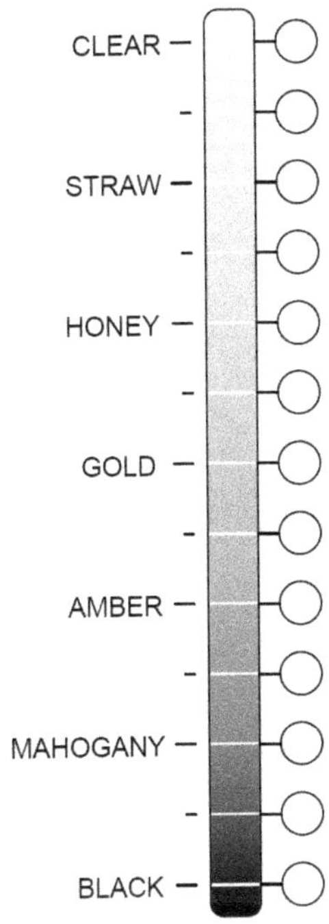

FLAVOR WHEEL

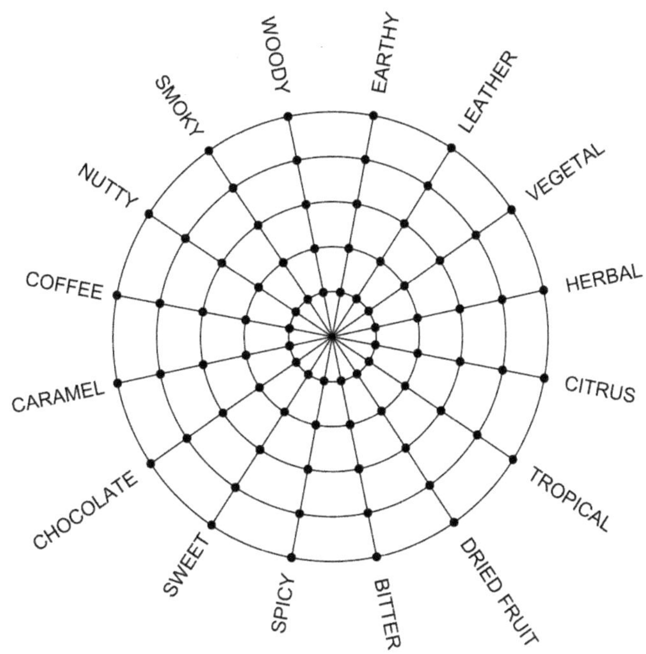

ADDITIONAL NOTES

FINAL RATING

APPEARANCE ☆☆☆☆☆

TASTE ☆☆☆☆☆

MOUTHFEEL ☆☆☆☆☆

OVERALL RATING ☆☆☆☆☆

NAME

DISTILLERY

TYPE

ORIGIN

AGE

PRICE

SAMPLED

COLOR METER

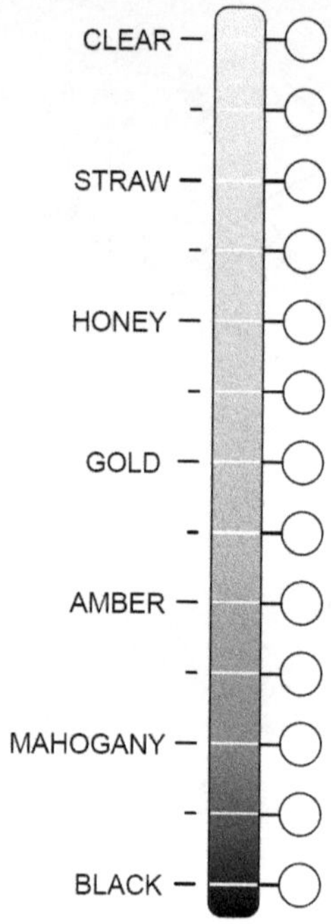

FLAVOR WHEEL

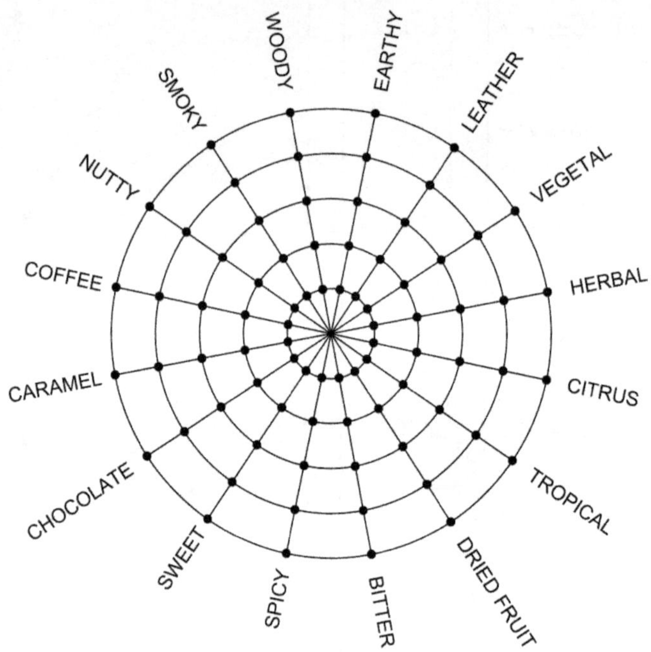

ADDITIONAL NOTES

FINAL RATING

APPEARANCE ☆☆☆☆☆

TASTE ☆☆☆☆☆

MOUTHFEEL ☆☆☆☆☆

OVERALL RATING ☆☆☆☆☆

NAME	
DISTILLERY	TYPE
ORIGIN	AGE
PRICE	SAMPLED

COLOR METER

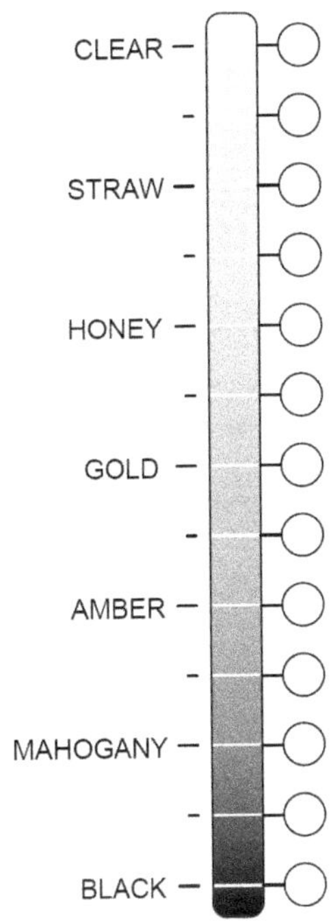

FLAVOR WHEEL

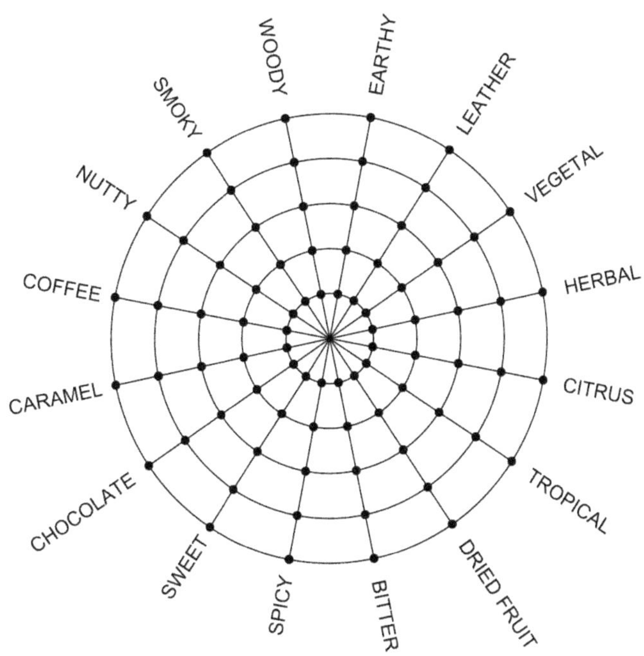

ADDITIONAL NOTES

FINAL RATING

APPEARANCE	☆☆☆☆☆
TASTE	☆☆☆☆☆
MOUTHFEEL	☆☆☆☆☆
OVERALL RATING	☆☆☆☆☆

NAME	
DISTILLERY	TYPE
ORIGIN	AGE
PRICE	SAMPLED

COLOR METER

- CLEAR
- STRAW
- HONEY
- GOLD
- AMBER
- MAHOGANY
- BLACK

FLAVOR WHEEL

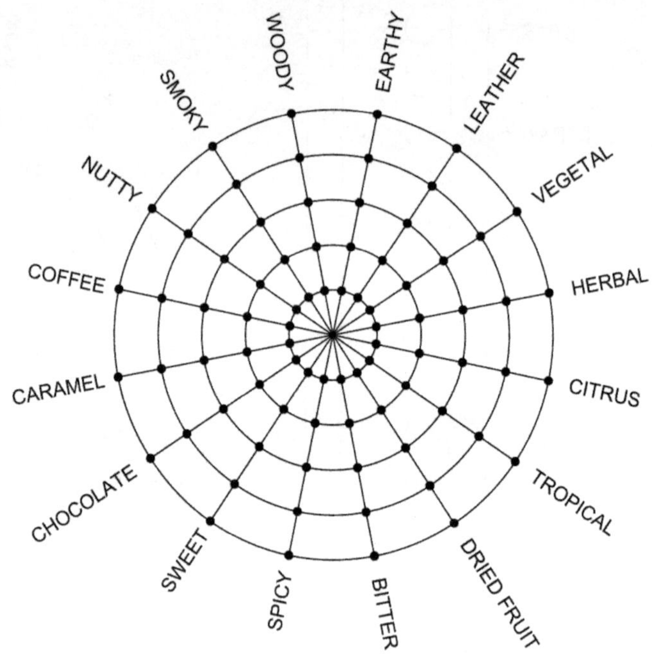

ADDITIONAL NOTES

FINAL RATING

APPEARANCE	☆☆☆☆☆
TASTE	☆☆☆☆☆
MOUTHFEEL	☆☆☆☆☆
OVERALL RATING	☆☆☆☆☆

NAME

DISTILLERY	TYPE
ORIGIN	AGE
PRICE	SAMPLED

COLOR METER

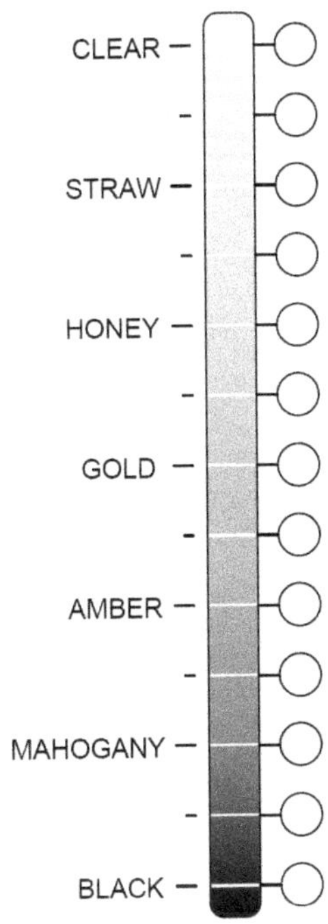

FLAVOR WHEEL

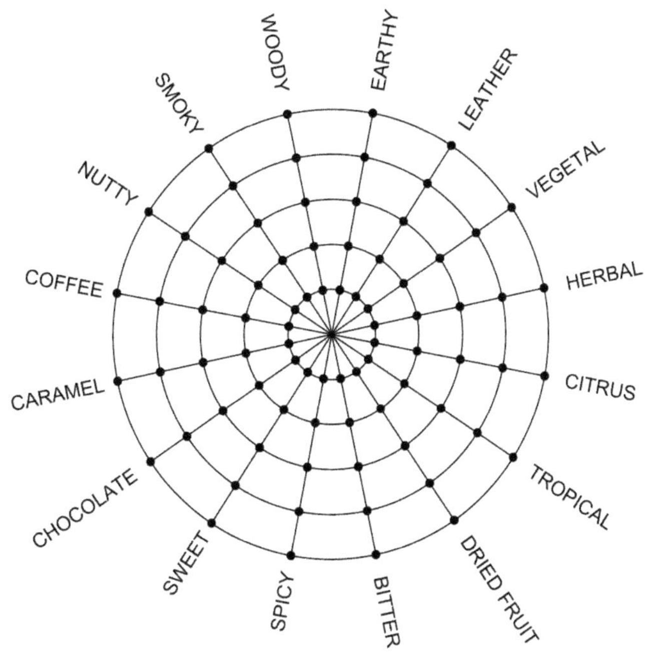

ADDITIONAL NOTES

FINAL RATING

APPEARANCE ☆☆☆☆☆

TASTE ☆☆☆☆☆

MOUTHFEEL ☆☆☆☆☆

OVERALL RATING ☆☆☆☆☆

NAME	
DISTILLERY	TYPE
ORIGIN	AGE
PRICE	SAMPLED

COLOR METER

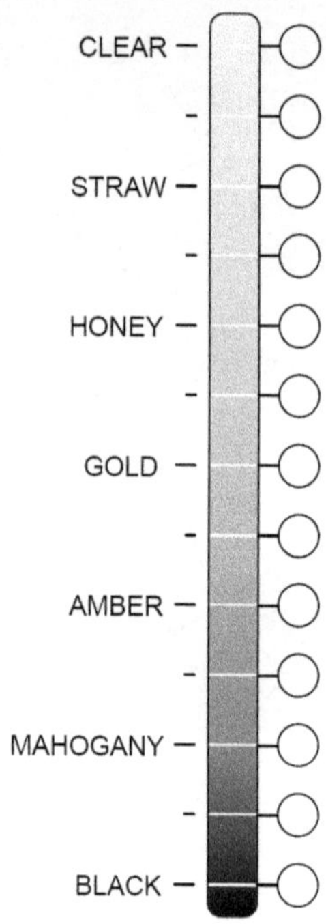

FLAVOR WHEEL

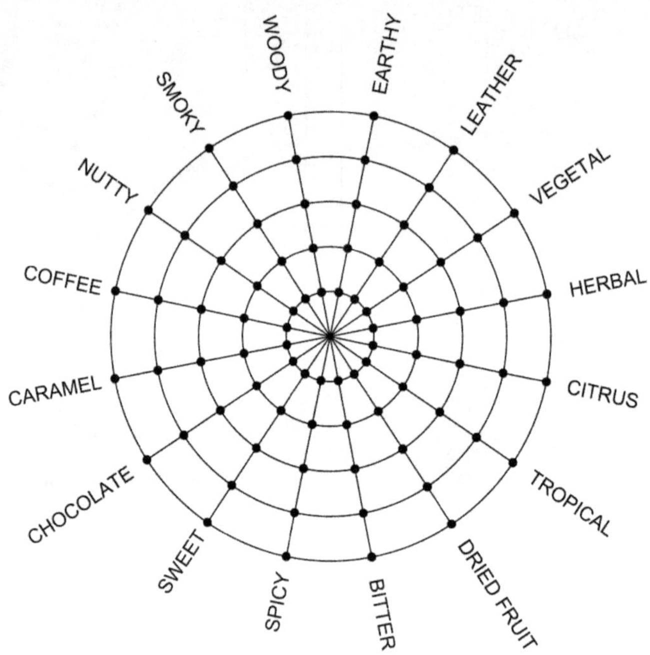

ADDITIONAL NOTES

FINAL RATING

APPEARANCE	☆☆☆☆☆
TASTE	☆☆☆☆☆
MOUTHFEEL	☆☆☆☆☆
OVERALL RATING	☆☆☆☆☆

NAME	
DISTILLERY	TYPE
ORIGIN	AGE
PRICE	SAMPLED

COLOR METER

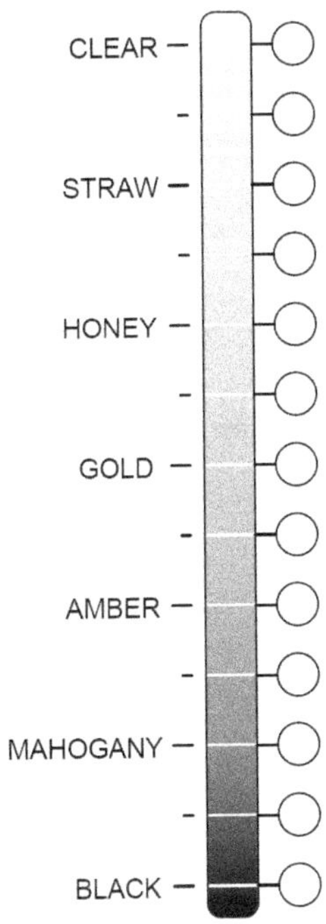

FLAVOR WHEEL

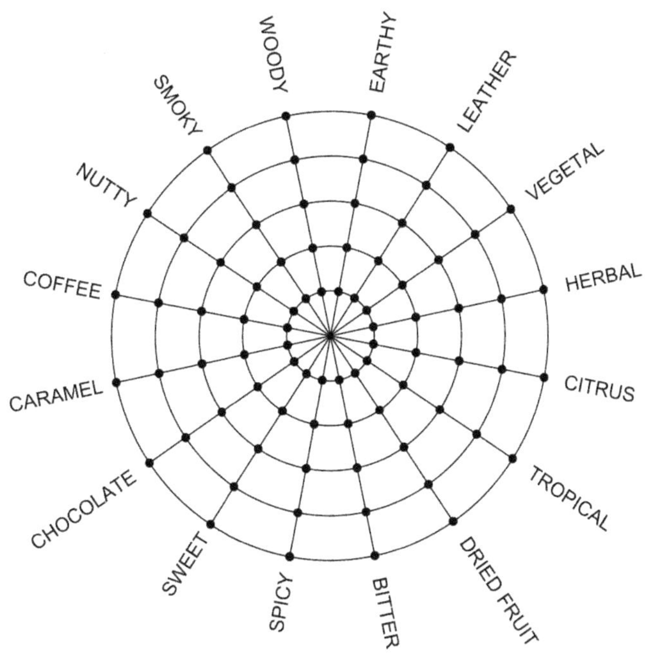

ADDITIONAL NOTES

FINAL RATING

APPEARANCE ☆☆☆☆☆

TASTE ☆☆☆☆☆

MOUTHFEEL ☆☆☆☆☆

OVERALL RATING ☆☆☆☆☆

NAME

DISTILLERY | TYPE

ORIGIN | AGE

PRICE | SAMPLED

COLOR METER

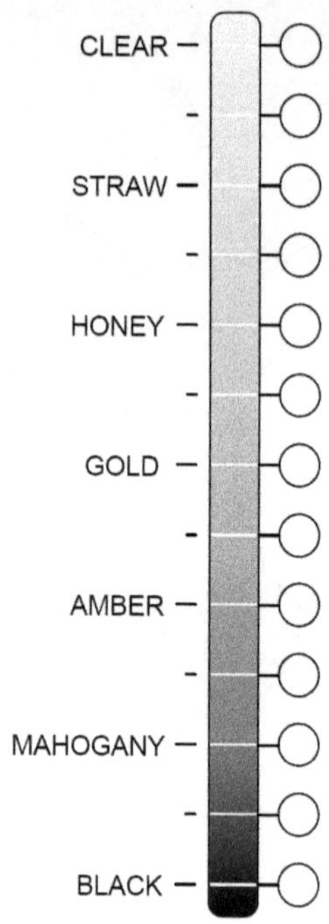

FLAVOR WHEEL

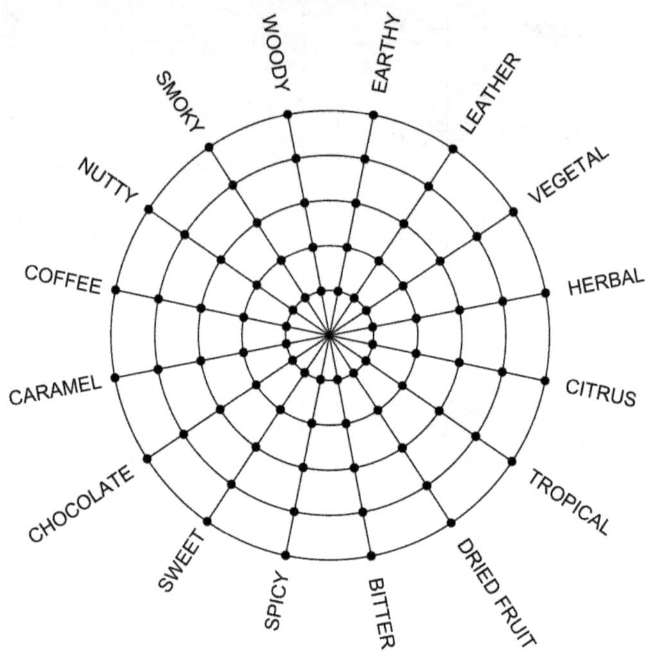

ADDITIONAL NOTES

FINAL RATING

APPEARANCE ☆☆☆☆☆

TASTE ☆☆☆☆☆

MOUTHFEEL ☆☆☆☆☆

OVERALL RATING ☆☆☆☆☆

NAME

DISTILLERY

TYPE

ORIGIN

AGE

PRICE

SAMPLED

COLOR METER

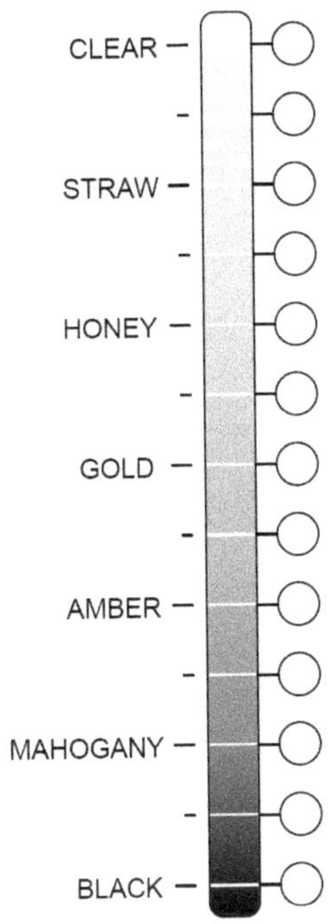

FLAVOR WHEEL

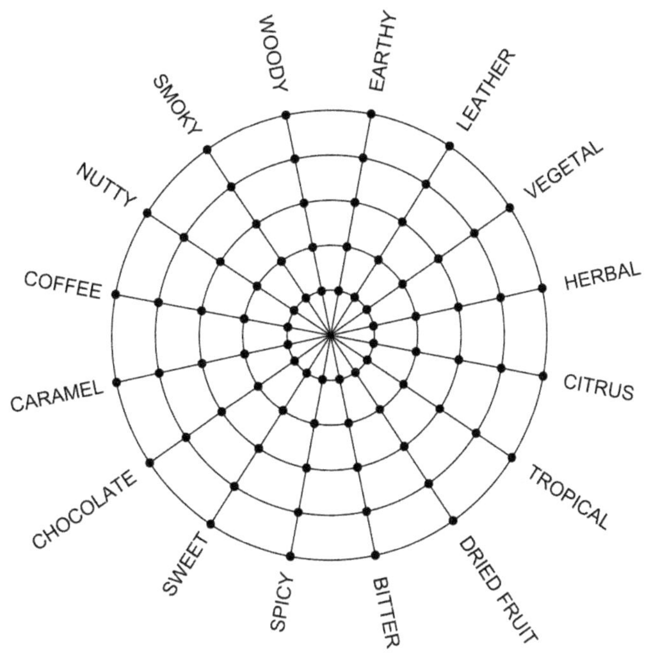

ADDITIONAL NOTES

FINAL RATING

APPEARANCE ☆☆☆☆☆

TASTE ☆☆☆☆☆

MOUTHFEEL ☆☆☆☆☆

OVERALL RATING ☆☆☆☆☆

NAME	
DISTILLERY	TYPE
ORIGIN	AGE
PRICE	SAMPLED

COLOR METER

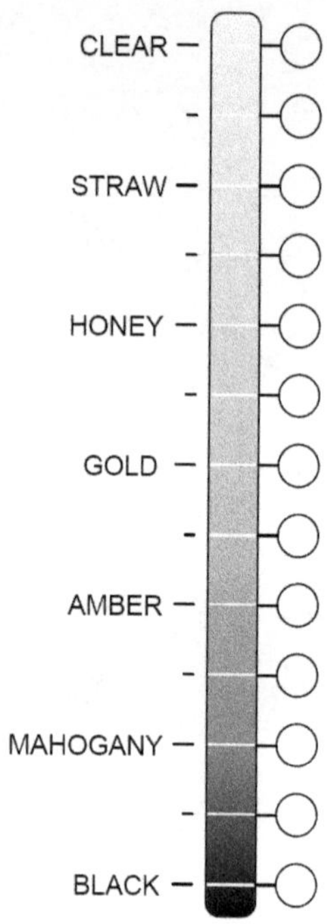

FLAVOR WHEEL

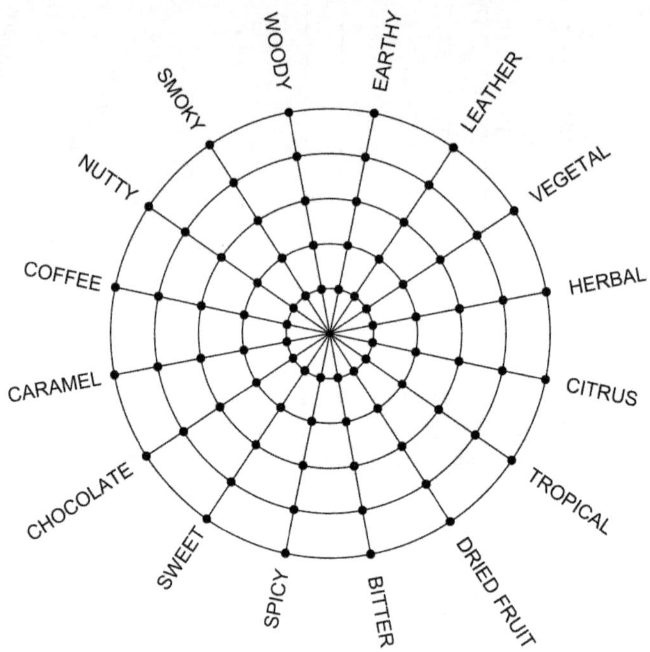

ADDITIONAL NOTES

FINAL RATING

APPEARANCE	☆☆☆☆☆
TASTE	☆☆☆☆☆
MOUTHFEEL	☆☆☆☆☆
OVERALL RATING	☆☆☆☆☆

NAME

DISTILLERY

TYPE

ORIGIN

AGE

PRICE

SAMPLED

COLOR METER

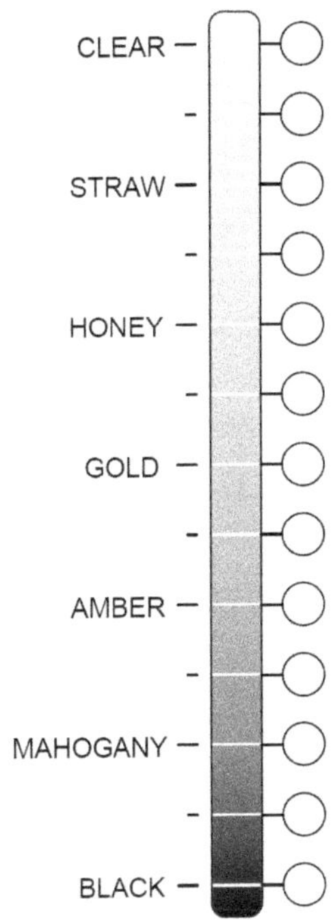

FLAVOR WHEEL

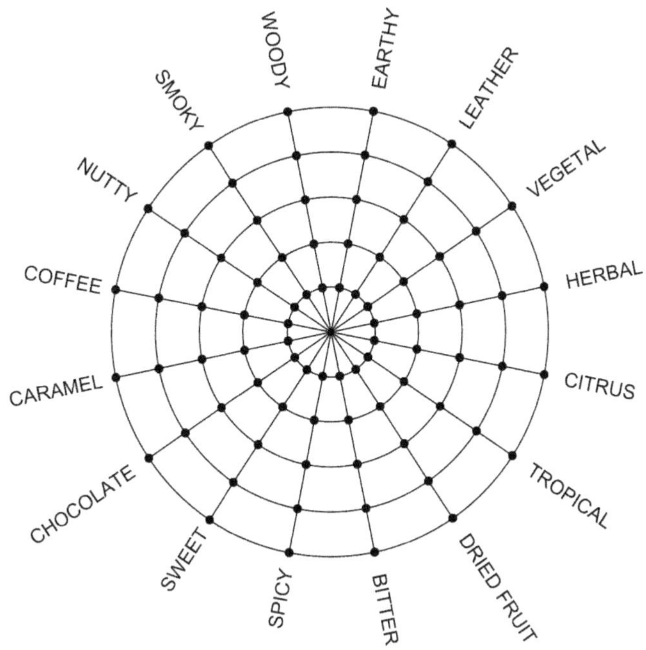

ADDITIONAL NOTES

FINAL RATING

APPEARANCE ☆☆☆☆☆

TASTE ☆☆☆☆☆

MOUTHFEEL ☆☆☆☆☆

OVERALL RATING ☆☆☆☆☆

NAME

DISTILLERY

TYPE

ORIGIN

AGE

PRICE

SAMPLED

COLOR METER

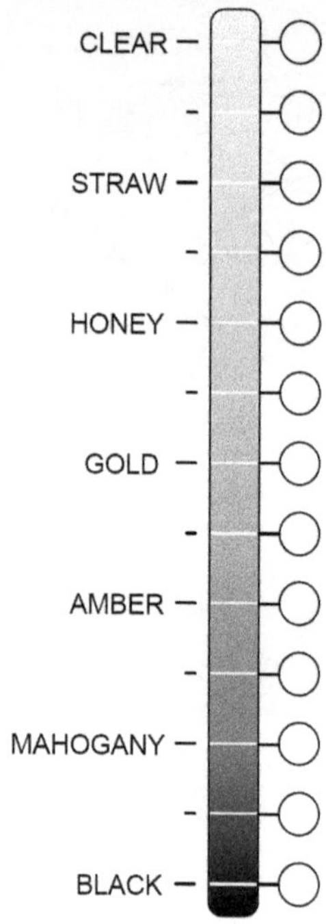

FLAVOR WHEEL

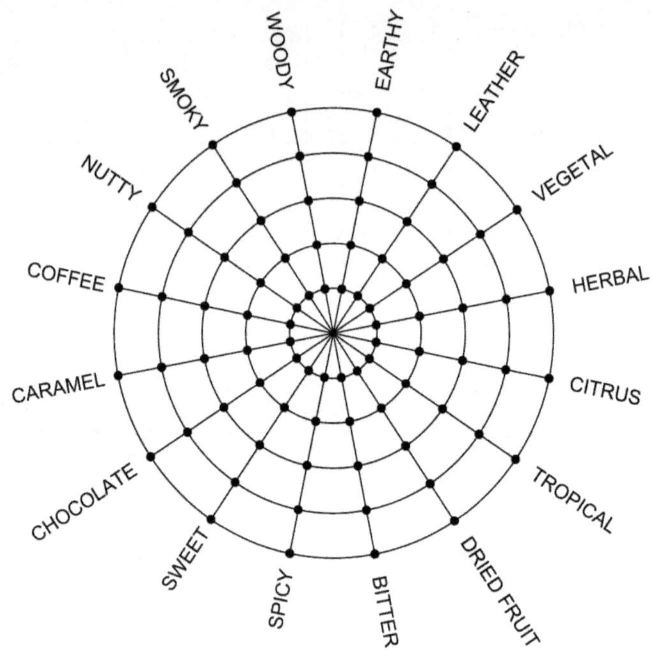

ADDITIONAL NOTES

FINAL RATING

APPEARANCE	☆☆☆☆☆
TASTE	☆☆☆☆☆
MOUTHFEEL	☆☆☆☆☆
OVERALL RATING	☆☆☆☆☆

NAME

DISTILLERY	TYPE
ORIGIN	AGE
PRICE	SAMPLED

COLOR METER

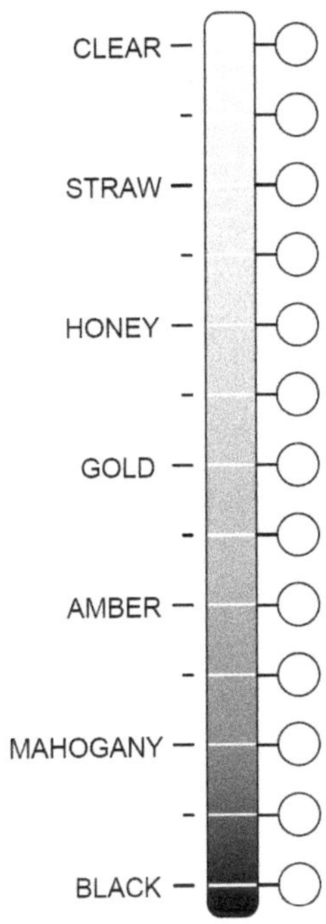

FLAVOR WHEEL

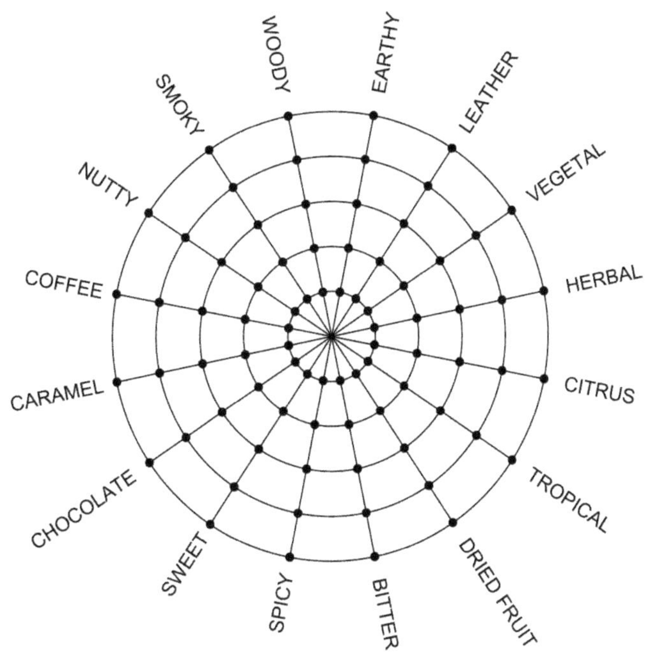

ADDITIONAL NOTES

FINAL RATING

APPEARANCE ☆☆☆☆☆

TASTE ☆☆☆☆☆

MOUTHFEEL ☆☆☆☆☆

OVERALL RATING ☆☆☆☆☆

NAME

DISTILLERY | TYPE

ORIGIN | AGE

PRICE | SAMPLED

COLOR METER

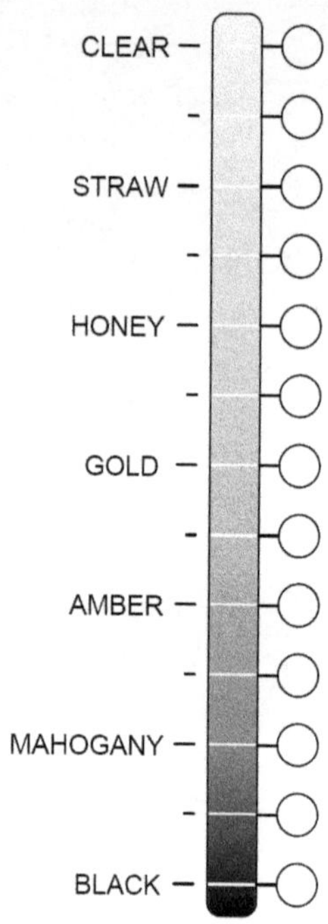

FLAVOR WHEEL

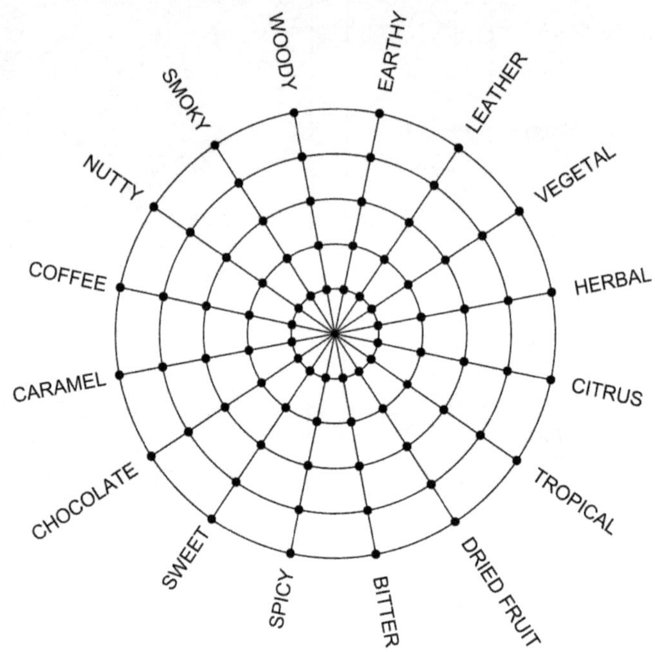

ADDITIONAL NOTES

FINAL RATING

APPEARANCE ☆☆☆☆☆

TASTE ☆☆☆☆☆

MOUTHFEEL ☆☆☆☆☆

OVERALL RATING ☆☆☆☆☆

NAME

DISTILLERY

TYPE

ORIGIN

AGE

PRICE

SAMPLED

COLOR METER

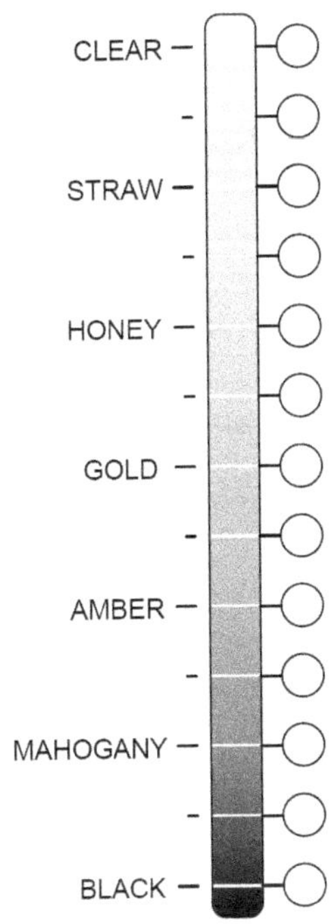

FLAVOR WHEEL

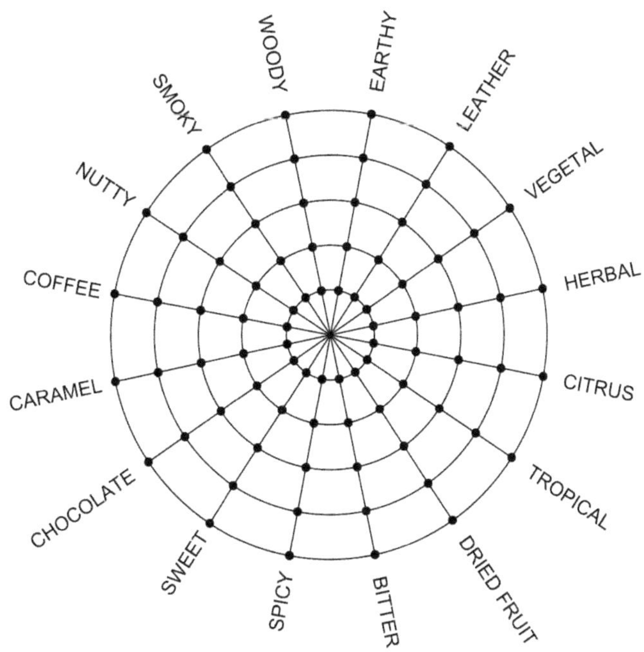

ADDITIONAL NOTES

FINAL RATING

APPEARANCE ☆☆☆☆☆

TASTE ☆☆☆☆☆

MOUTHFEEL ☆☆☆☆☆

OVERALL RATING ☆☆☆☆☆

NAME	
DISTILLERY	TYPE
ORIGIN	AGE
PRICE	SAMPLED

COLOR METER

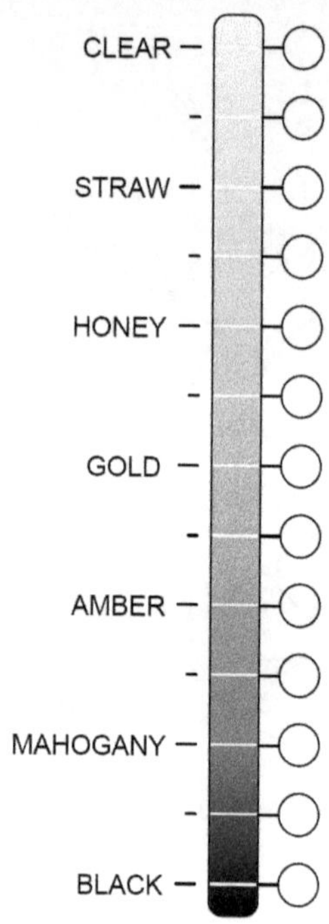

FLAVOR WHEEL

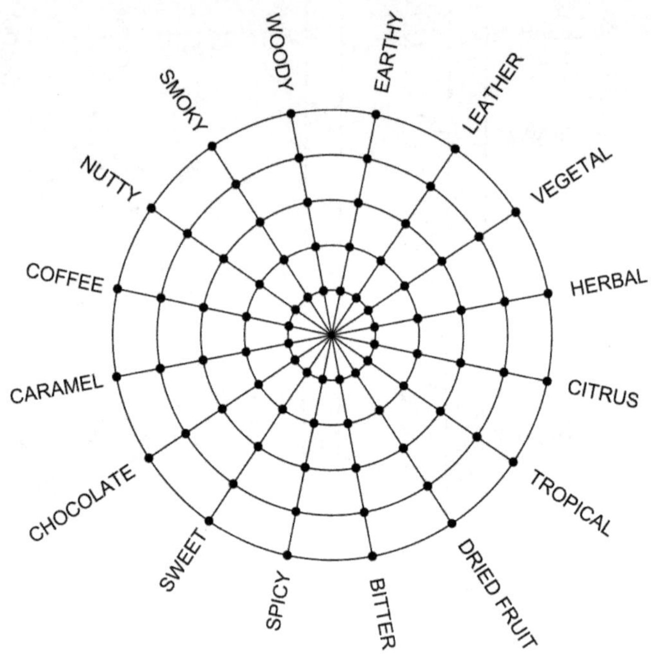

ADDITIONAL NOTES

FINAL RATING

APPEARANCE	☆☆☆☆☆
TASTE	☆☆☆☆☆
MOUTHFEEL	☆☆☆☆☆
OVERALL RATING	☆☆☆☆☆

NAME	
DISTILLERY	TYPE
ORIGIN	AGE
PRICE	SAMPLED

COLOR METER

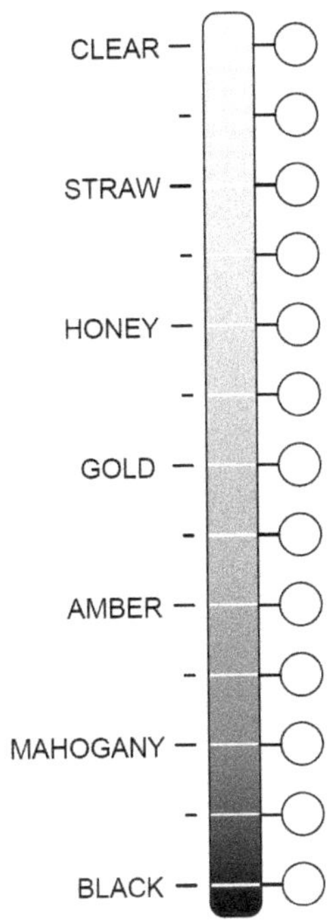

FLAVOR WHEEL

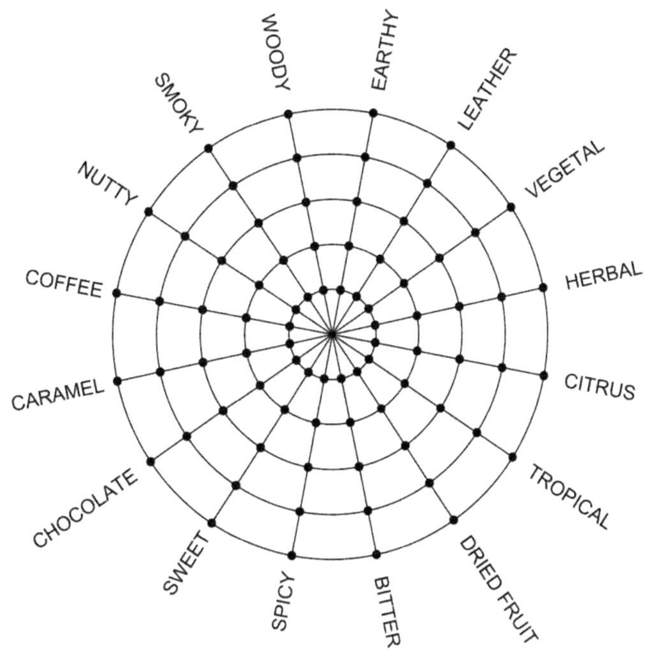

ADDITIONAL NOTES

FINAL RATING

APPEARANCE	☆☆☆☆☆
TASTE	☆☆☆☆☆
MOUTHFEEL	☆☆☆☆☆
OVERALL RATING	☆☆☆☆☆

NAME

DISTILLERY | TYPE

ORIGIN | AGE

PRICE | SAMPLED

COLOR METER

CLEAR
STRAW
HONEY
GOLD
AMBER
MAHOGANY
BLACK

FLAVOR WHEEL

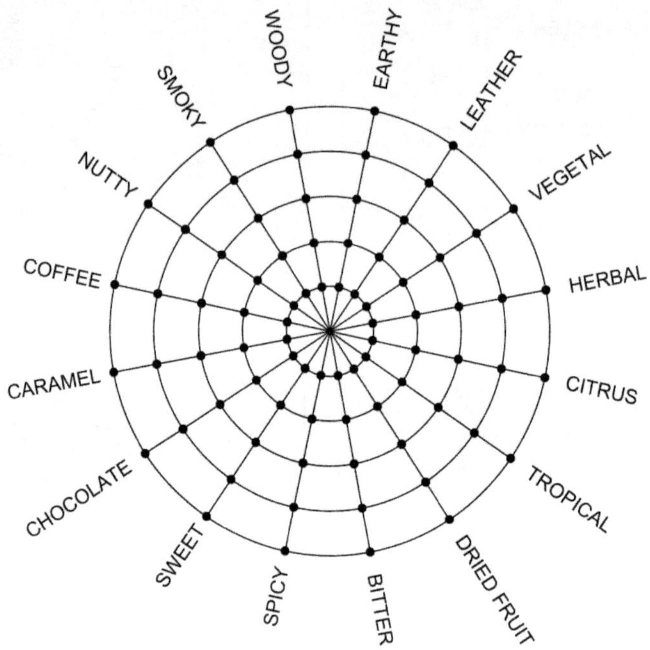

ADDITIONAL NOTES

FINAL RATING

APPEARANCE ☆☆☆☆☆

TASTE ☆☆☆☆☆

MOUTHFEEL ☆☆☆☆☆

OVERALL RATING ☆☆☆☆☆

NAME

DISTILLERY

TYPE

ORIGIN

AGE

PRICE

SAMPLED

COLOR METER

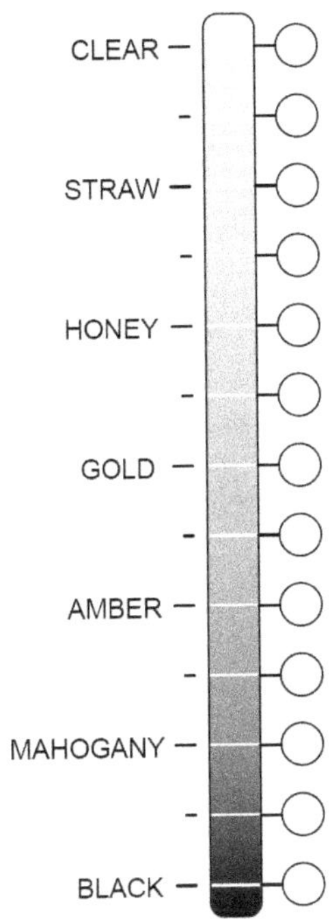

FLAVOR WHEEL

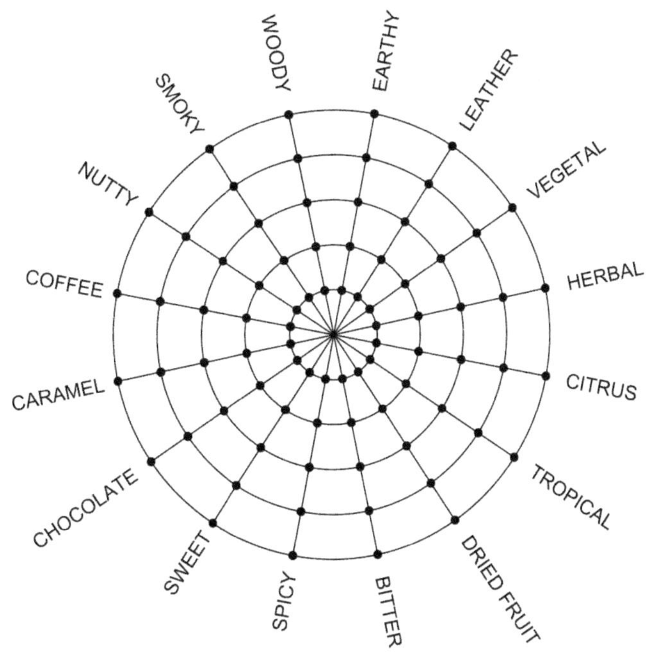

ADDITIONAL NOTES

FINAL RATING

APPEARANCE ☆☆☆☆☆

TASTE ☆☆☆☆☆

MOUTHFEEL ☆☆☆☆☆

OVERALL RATING ☆☆☆☆☆

NAME	
DISTILLERY	TYPE
ORIGIN	AGE
PRICE	SAMPLED

COLOR METER

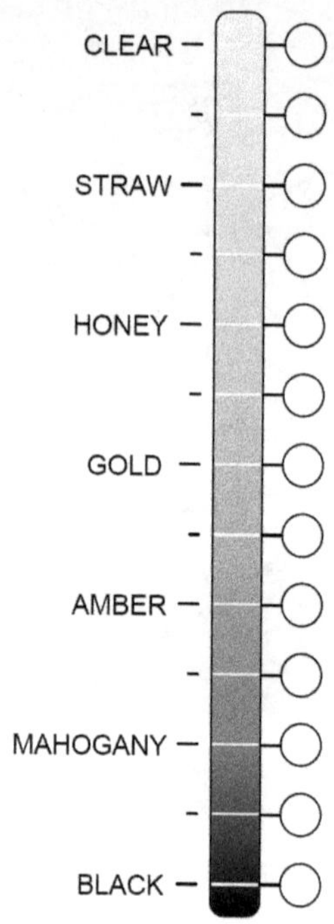

FLAVOR WHEEL

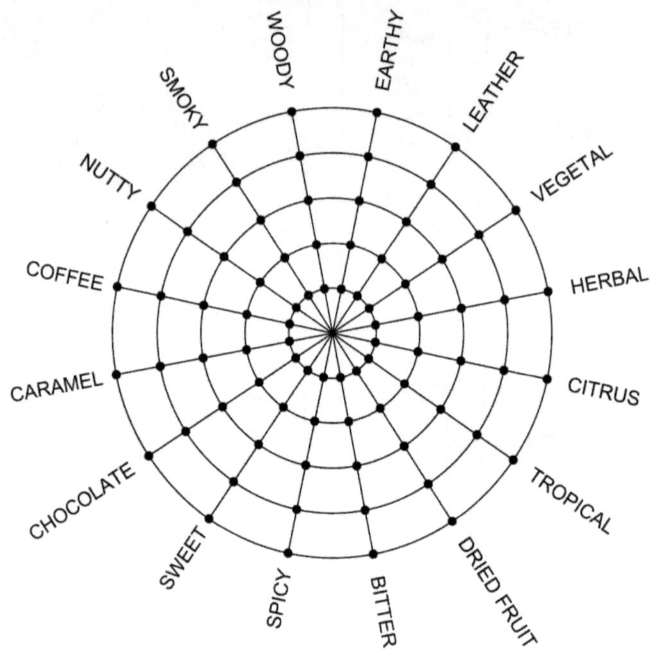

ADDITIONAL NOTES

FINAL RATING

APPEARANCE	☆☆☆☆☆
TASTE	☆☆☆☆☆
MOUTHFEEL	☆☆☆☆☆
OVERALL RATING	☆☆☆☆☆

NAME	
DISTILLERY	TYPE
ORIGIN	AGE
PRICE	SAMPLED

COLOR METER

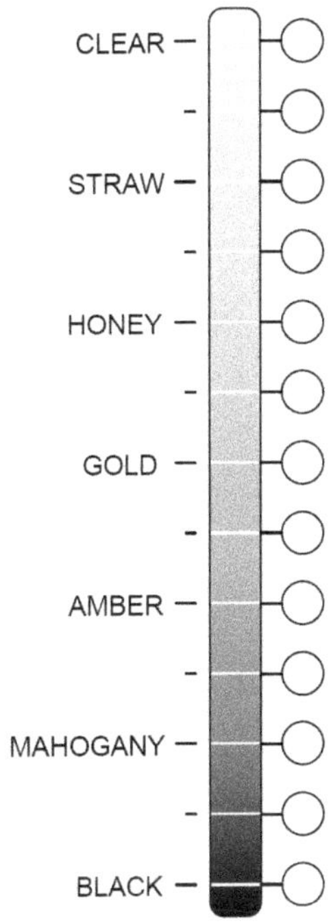

FLAVOR WHEEL

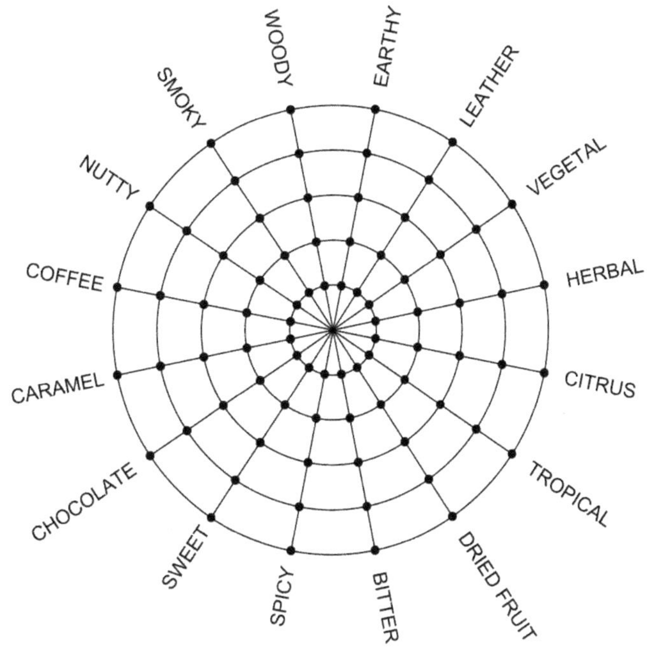

ADDITIONAL NOTES

FINAL RATING

APPEARANCE	☆☆☆☆☆
TASTE	☆☆☆☆☆
MOUTHFEEL	☆☆☆☆☆
OVERALL RATING	☆☆☆☆☆

NAME	
DISTILLERY	TYPE
ORIGIN	AGE
PRICE	SAMPLED

COLOR METER

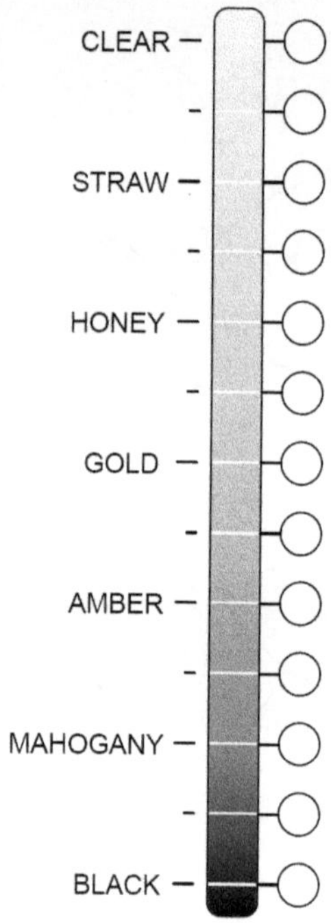

FLAVOR WHEEL

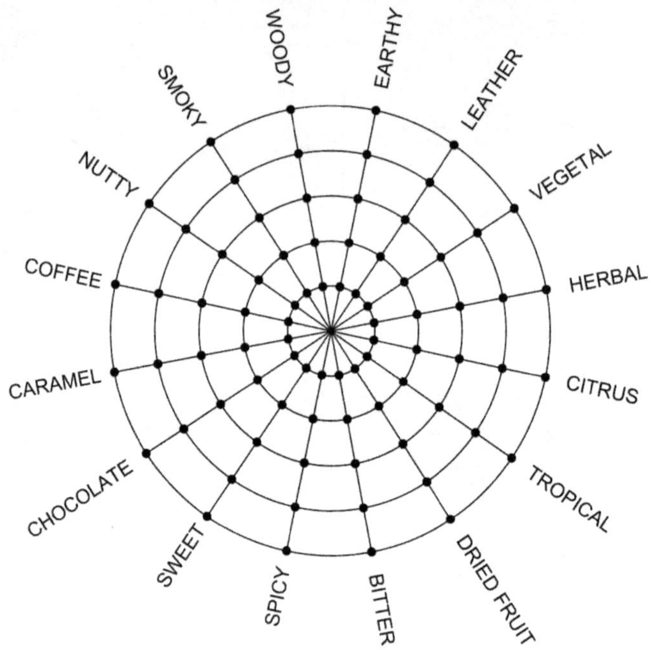

ADDITIONAL NOTES

FINAL RATING

APPEARANCE ☆☆☆☆☆

TASTE ☆☆☆☆☆

MOUTHFEEL ☆☆☆☆☆

OVERALL RATING ☆☆☆☆☆

NAME

DISTILLERY

TYPE

ORIGIN

AGE

PRICE

SAMPLED

COLOR METER

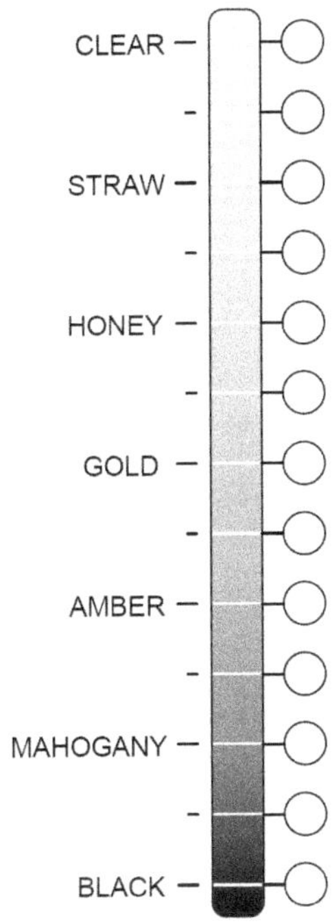

FLAVOR WHEEL

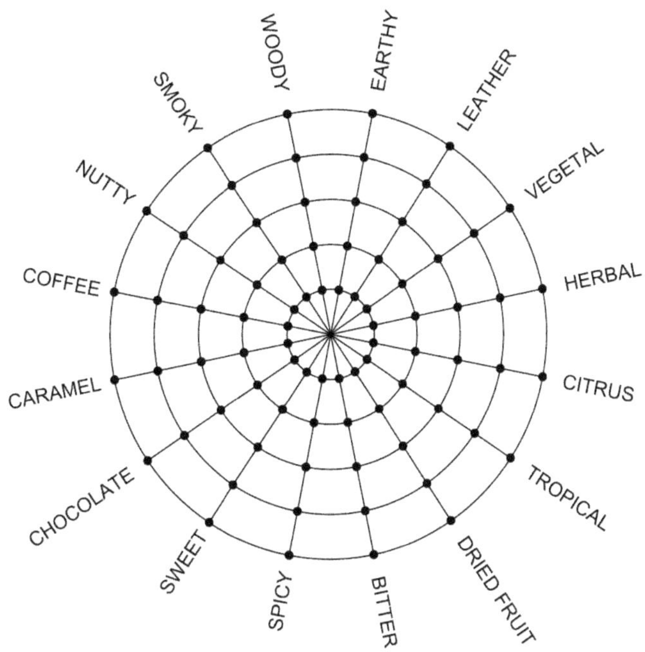

ADDITIONAL NOTES

FINAL RATING

APPEARANCE ☆☆☆☆☆

TASTE ☆☆☆☆☆

MOUTHFEEL ☆☆☆☆☆

OVERALL RATING ☆☆☆☆☆

NAME

DISTILLERY

TYPE

ORIGIN

AGE

PRICE

SAMPLED

COLOR METER

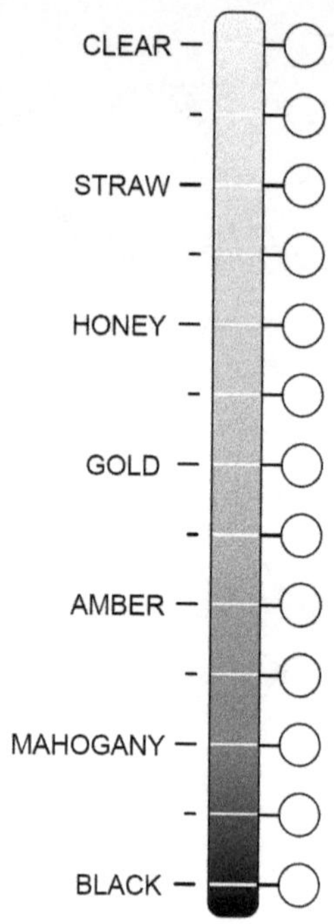

FLAVOR WHEEL

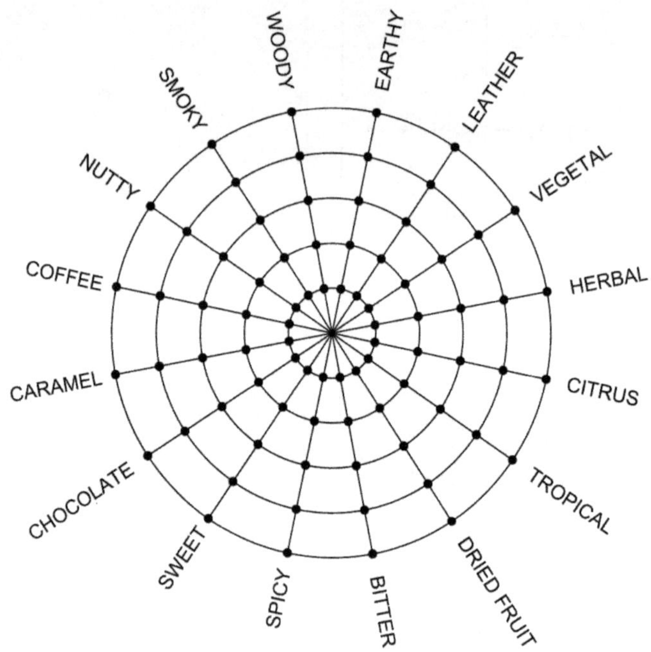

ADDITIONAL NOTES

FINAL RATING

APPEARANCE ☆☆☆☆☆

TASTE ☆☆☆☆☆

MOUTHFEEL ☆☆☆☆☆

OVERALL RATING ☆☆☆☆☆

NAME	
DISTILLERY	TYPE
ORIGIN	AGE
PRICE	SAMPLED

COLOR METER

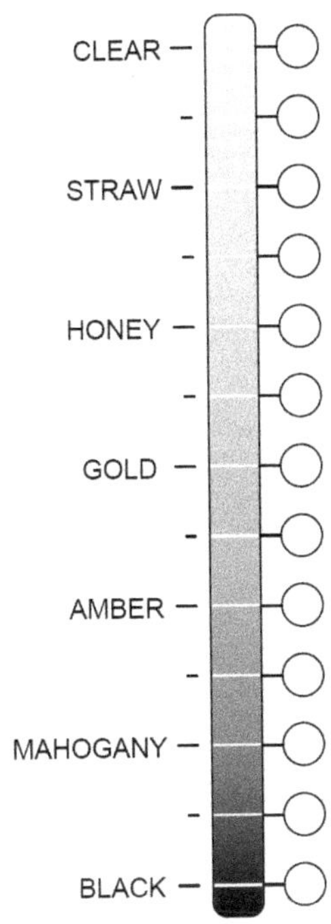

FLAVOR WHEEL

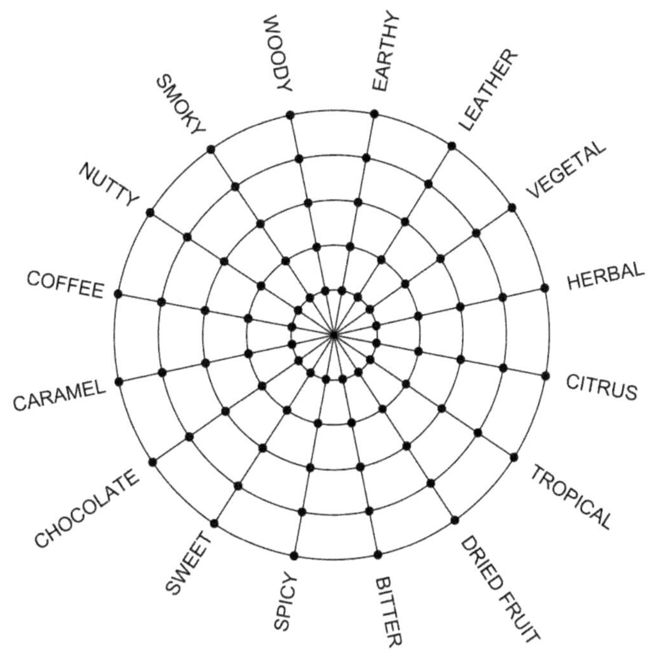

ADDITIONAL NOTES

FINAL RATING

APPEARANCE	☆☆☆☆☆
TASTE	☆☆☆☆☆
MOUTHFEEL	☆☆☆☆☆
OVERALL RATING	☆☆☆☆☆

NAME	
DISTILLERY	TYPE
ORIGIN	AGE
PRICE	SAMPLED

COLOR METER

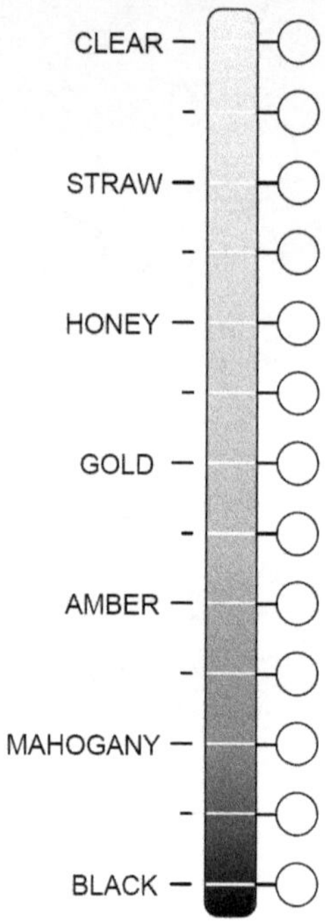

FLAVOR WHEEL

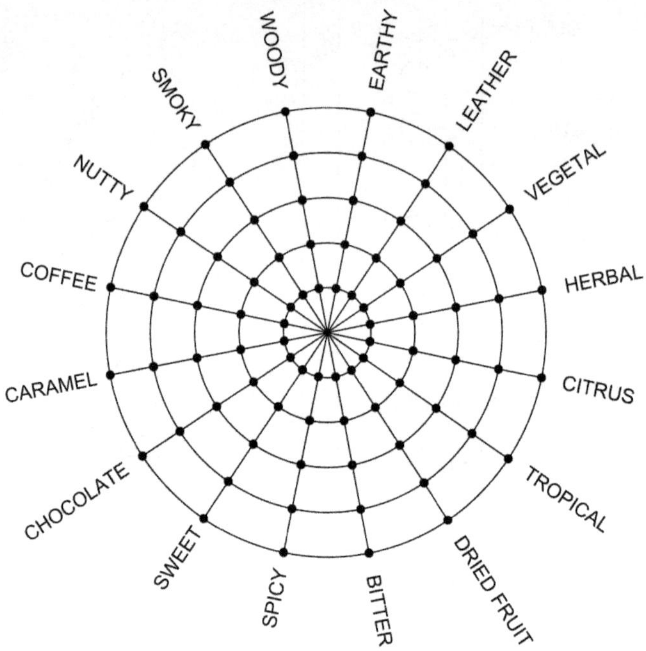

ADDITIONAL NOTES

FINAL RATING

APPEARANCE	☆☆☆☆☆
TASTE	☆☆☆☆☆
MOUTHFEEL	☆☆☆☆☆
OVERALL RATING	☆☆☆☆☆

NAME	
DISTILLERY	TYPE
ORIGIN	AGE
PRICE	SAMPLED

COLOR METER

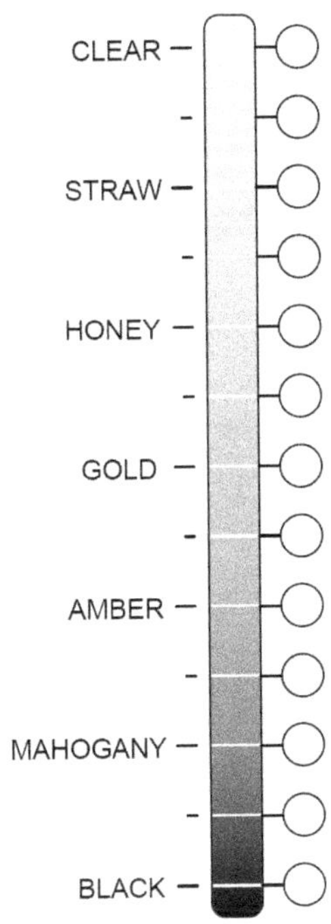

FLAVOR WHEEL

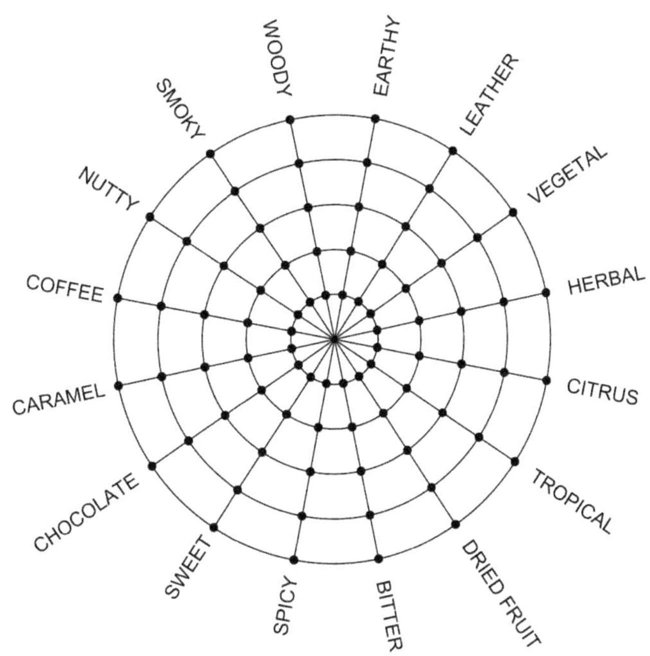

ADDITIONAL NOTES

FINAL RATING

APPEARANCE	☆☆☆☆☆
TASTE	☆☆☆☆☆
MOUTHFEEL	☆☆☆☆☆
OVERALL RATING	☆☆☆☆☆

NAME

DISTILLERY | TYPE

ORIGIN | AGE

PRICE | SAMPLED

COLOR METER

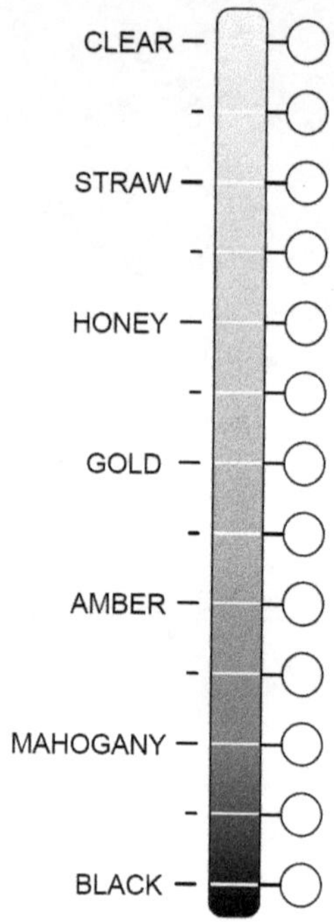

FLAVOR WHEEL

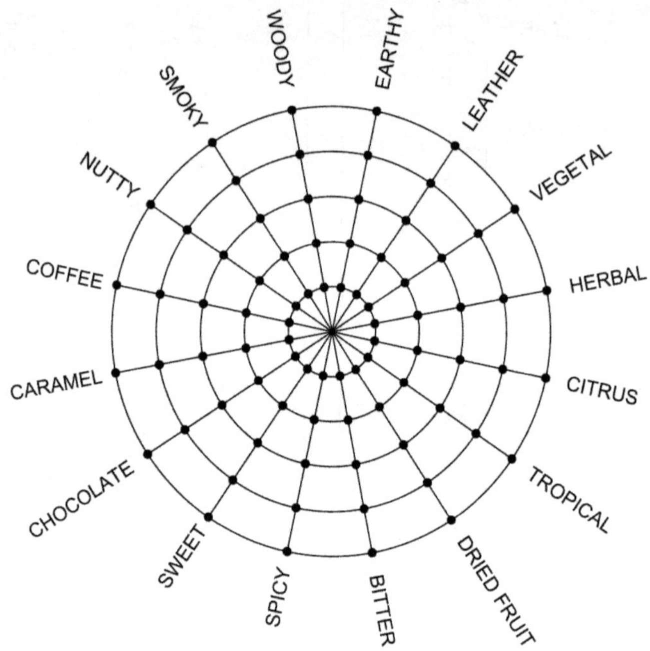

ADDITIONAL NOTES

FINAL RATING

APPEARANCE	☆☆☆☆☆
TASTE	☆☆☆☆☆
MOUTHFEEL	☆☆☆☆☆
OVERALL RATING	☆☆☆☆☆

NAME	
DISTILLERY	TYPE
ORIGIN	AGE
PRICE	SAMPLED

COLOR METER

CLEAR
STRAW
HONEY
GOLD
AMBER
MAHOGANY
BLACK

FLAVOR WHEEL

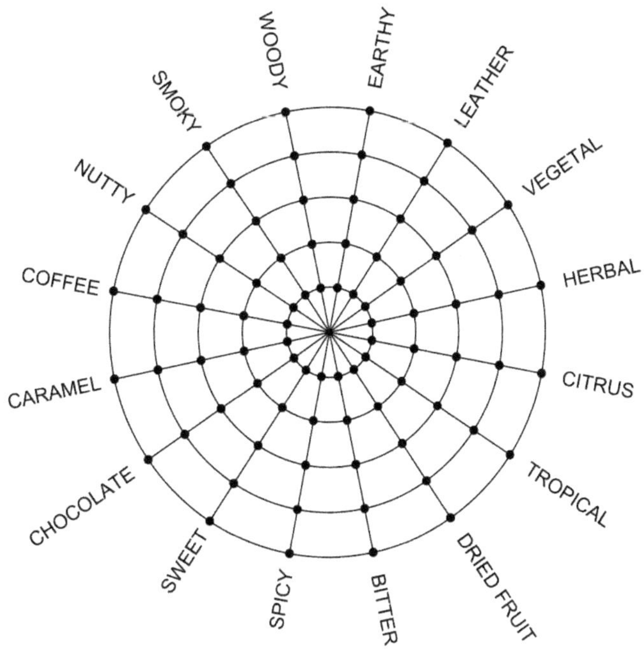

ADDITIONAL NOTES

FINAL RATING

APPEARANCE ☆☆☆☆☆
TASTE ☆☆☆☆☆
MOUTHFEEL ☆☆☆☆☆
OVERALL RATING ☆☆☆☆☆

NAME	
DISTILLERY	TYPE
ORIGIN	AGE
PRICE	SAMPLED

COLOR METER

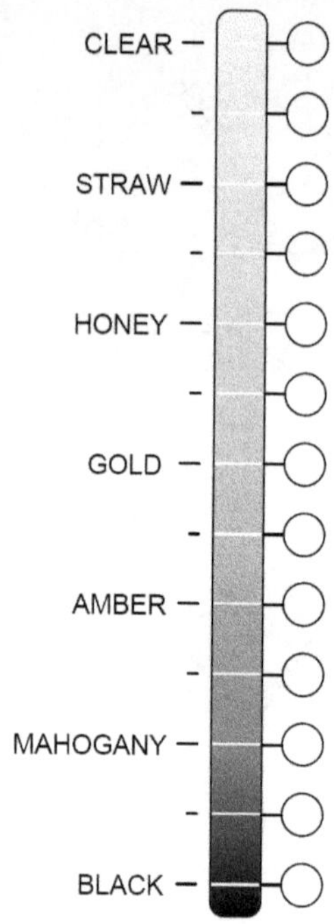

FLAVOR WHEEL

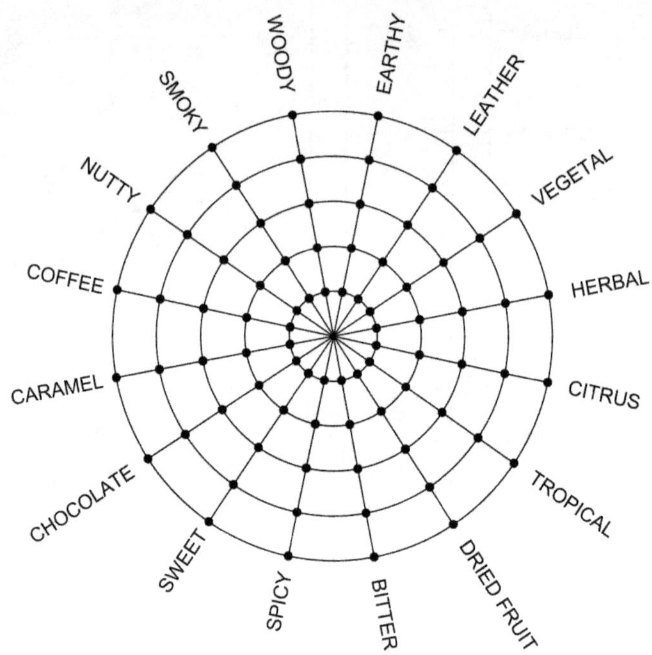

ADDITIONAL NOTES

FINAL RATING

APPEARANCE ☆☆☆☆☆

TASTE ☆☆☆☆☆

MOUTHFEEL ☆☆☆☆☆

OVERALL RATING ☆☆☆☆☆

NAME

DISTILLERY	TYPE
ORIGIN	AGE
PRICE	SAMPLED

COLOR METER

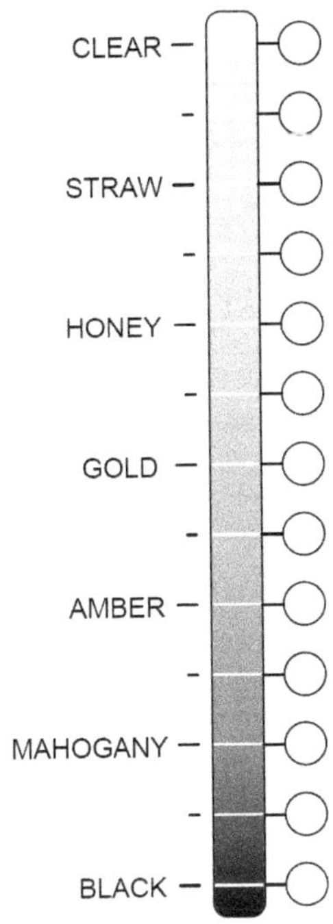

FLAVOR WHEEL

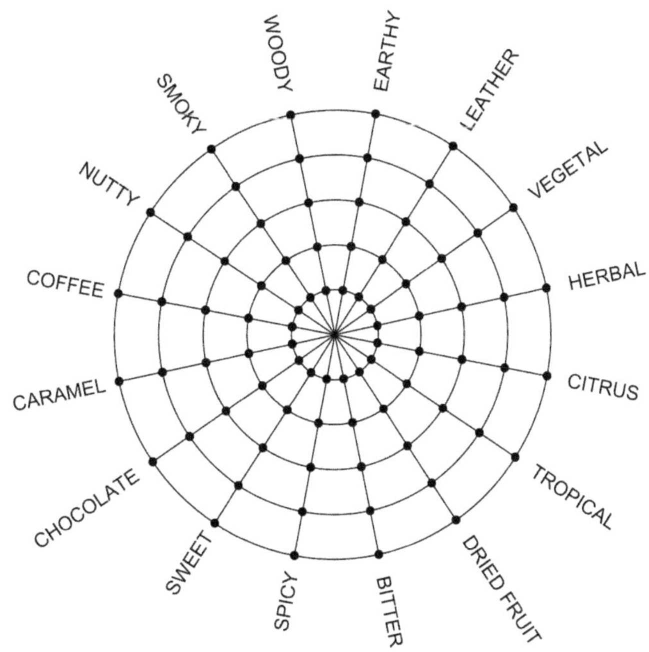

ADDITIONAL NOTES

FINAL RATING

APPEARANCE	☆☆☆☆☆
TASTE	☆☆☆☆☆
MOUTHFEEL	☆☆☆☆☆
OVERALL RATING	☆☆☆☆☆

NAME

DISTILLERY

TYPE

ORIGIN

AGE

PRICE

SAMPLED

COLOR METER

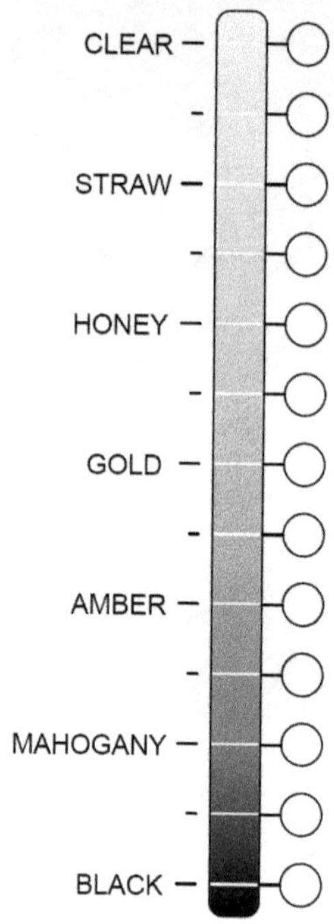

FLAVOR WHEEL

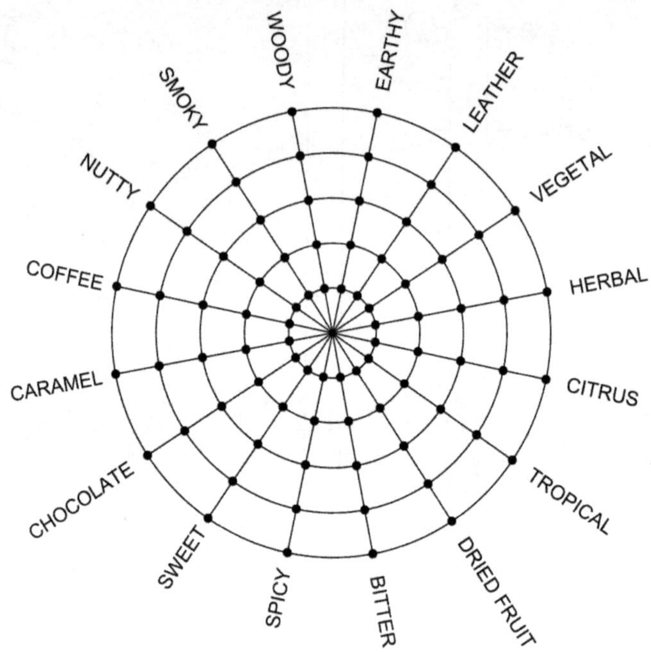

ADDITIONAL NOTES

FINAL RATING

APPEARANCE	☆☆☆☆☆
TASTE	☆☆☆☆☆
MOUTHFEEL	☆☆☆☆☆
OVERALL RATING	☆☆☆☆☆

NAME	
DISTILLERY	TYPE
ORIGIN	AGE
PRICE	SAMPLED

COLOR METER

- CLEAR
- STRAW
- HONEY
- GOLD
- AMBER
- MAHOGANY
- BLACK

FLAVOR WHEEL

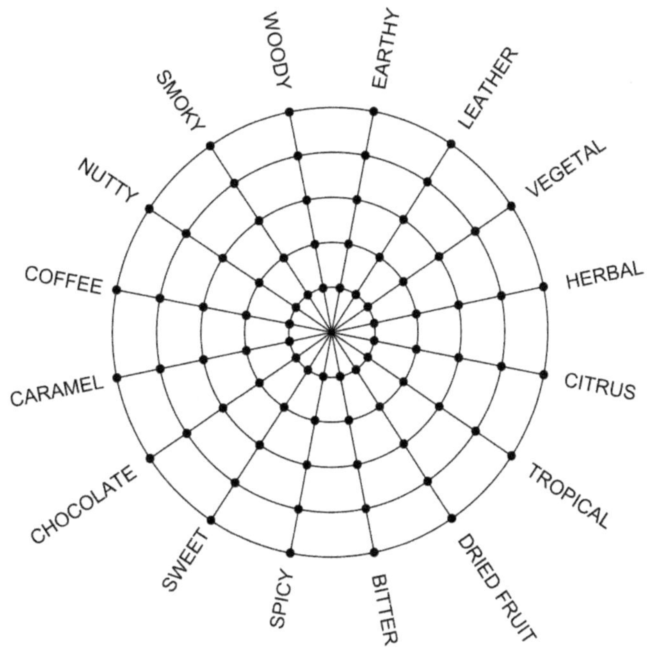

ADDITIONAL NOTES

FINAL RATING

APPEARANCE	☆☆☆☆☆
TASTE	☆☆☆☆☆
MOUTHFEEL	☆☆☆☆☆
OVERALL RATING	☆☆☆☆☆

NAME

DISTILLERY

TYPE

ORIGIN

AGE

PRICE

SAMPLED

COLOR METER

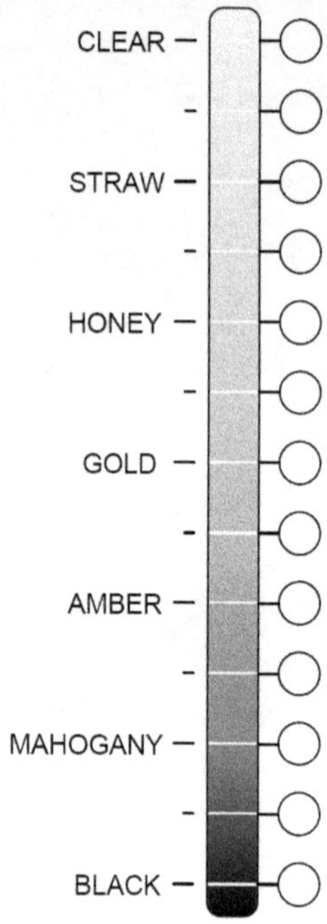

FLAVOR WHEEL

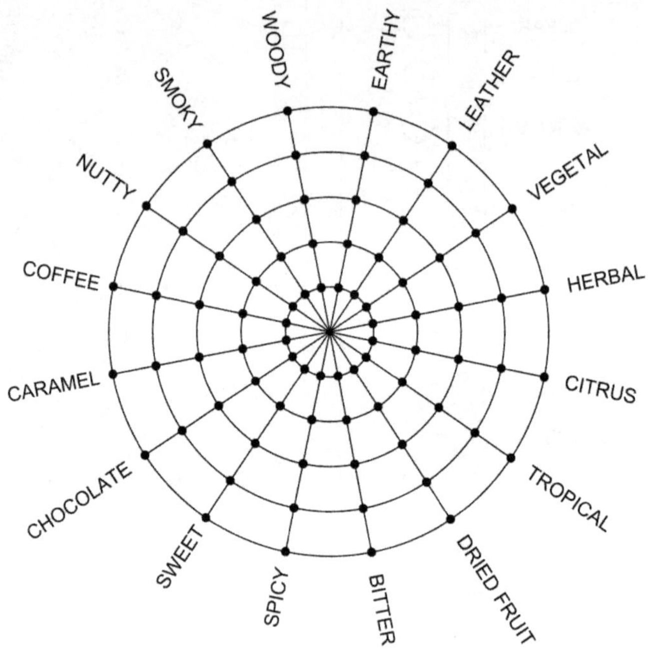

ADDITIONAL NOTES

FINAL RATING

APPEARANCE	☆☆☆☆☆
TASTE	☆☆☆☆☆
MOUTHFEEL	☆☆☆☆☆
OVERALL RATING	☆☆☆☆☆

Lightning Source UK Ltd.
Milton Keynes UK
UKHW051857070820
367798UK00006BD/749

9 781649 302762